Hope Ignited

Compiled by Brigitte Brown Jackson

Forward by Carla Allen

UBUNTU PRESS
PO BOX 524 Flint, MI 48501-0470
(810) 814-5464
www.ubuntupress.com

DEDICATION

Dedicated to one of the most hopeful people God created,
Shakila Gibson – BBJ

The contributors wish to dedicate this book to
all the women who have overcome and are overcoming.

CONTENTS

ACKNOWLEDGMENTS

We thank God for this work and the contributors who poured out their hearts and souls to deliver a message of hope. We wish to acknowledge them for giving of themselves and being transparent for the sake of helping other women in need. They are their sister's keepers—many of them sharing things that were not entirely told in whole to other audiences.

We want to thank Co-Pastor Carla Allen for her optimism and support. She always has an encouraging word. She is one of the most beautiful people in the world, always offering hope.

To all of the women who were a part of the 2021 Powerful: Ordained for It Virtual Conference, we were not able to capture your story in this edition, but your presence on stage blessed us during the conference. You are mighty, dynamic, influential women doing great exploits in the world to help bless others.

I want to acknowledge you. Yes, Y-O-U. The person who is reading this right now. I see you, sis. I affirm you for reading whether just to read to be better or if you are in a dark place, know you are not by yourself. YANA – you are not alone. You have a tribe of sisters that are here cheering you on in the midst of whatever you are hoping for.

While taking this book to publication, my beautiful, vibrant, loving, and caring niece, Shakila Gibson, went on to be with the Lord. She fought a good fight, and she kept the faith. She had a heart that hope flowed out of like curtains in an open window on a windy day. With her last breaths, she continued to praise God. She believed in God for her healing. For all those like Shakila – keep hoping. Whatever the thing is you are dealing with, just keep believing. Let nothing take away your hope. Shakila gave me hope on top of the hope I already possessed. I thought I could do all things, but now I have an even more profound sense of aspiration for God's mercy. Thank you, my beautiful niece, for your modeling of how to love and praise God.

Finally, I would be remiss if I didn't recognize my sister Shareefa Clark, I will continue to allow her legacy to live. She was such a giving soul. She possessed a heart of gold. She always walked in hope and lived a life serving others. As the younger sibling, she acted like the eldest in protecting me; she was my hero. Her life inspired me to start the woman's ministry I had been doing since her death in 1997. I KNOW I WILL see her on the great resurrection day, but I mostly hope to see her reflection in women I am so excited to serve.

Thank you to each person, ministry, or business that supported our presales before publication. Your kindness gave us *HOPE*!

Carla Allen
Michelle Robinson
Rochelle Schwartz
Alisha Schwartz
Maria Green
Destined to Heal, LLC
Getting Beauty for Our Ashes
Heather 'Byrd' Roberts
Rasath1
Trische Duckworth
Jacqueline McDaniel Vasquez
Cameasha Muhammad
Patricia Duckworth
Willie Jackson III
Karen Jones
Mischa Hardin
Dewaynia Howard
Delicate Beauty Skincare
LeTina Williams
Carol O'Banion
Adrian Spiller
SaRoya Morrison
Darcele - Donations With Love
Kimberly Pickett
Saharra James
Leah Mills
Kayla Wright
Quarlita Smith
C Morgan
Jaz'Min Nunnally
Sayonie Morgan
Tommie Holloway Jr.
HM Life Investments
Matthew Jackson
Dawn Kelly

Iris King
Barakah
Ihudiya Williams
Casanova Bowers
Matthew Jackson
Elizabeth Bailey
Lisa Querijo
Rakisha Johnson
Cynthia Hill
Jasmine Guin
Stephen Mackey
Delphine Jackson Rogers
Cheerese Smith
Shanice Brooks
Erica Hawkins
Samantha Gause
Tearia Williams
Robin Anderson
Tamika Mathis
Shanick Bartell
Sally Haines
Phyllis Dixon
Patricia Smith
Fatima Dixon
Bianca Avery/Boarding By Bianca
Tiffany Taxes
IMA Consulting
Kingdom Influence Ministries
TaNeya Hunter
LaMonica Lee
Pamela Burleigh
Tiffany Saunders
Valerie Fabre-Williams
Nicole Dixson-Mays
Donata Mooring

FORWARD

I am so honored to have been asked to write this forward. It brings me great joy to announce this book. This literary work is very essential and necessary for the healing of so many people in the world today.

The written content of *Hope Ignited: Stories of Hope for Women by Women* embodies a beautiful collaborative effort from some phenomenal women around the world. It's written for women by women through transparency. They are sharing from their hearts, minds, and life experiences.

If there has ever been a time in the world where so many people need their hope reignited, it is now! Because of the pandemic and the massive number of losses, many have suffered tremendously, and many people have found themselves in a state of hopelessness.

I believe this book should be distributed throughout the world because of its relevant content. Someone needs to know that there is still hope no matter the challenging situation they face in life!

There is always hope.

Upon the completion of reading this book, I assure you that your hope will be ignited, and your life and mindset will be forever changed. I firmly believe after enjoying *Hope Ignited;* your faith will be yearning to go on a new journey filled with faith. A journey in which includes the Lord Jesus Christ.

Hebrews 11:1 states,
> *"For faith is the substance of things hoped for, and the evidence of things not seen." (KJV)*

If you can envision it, pray, and believe God for it to come to pass.

As God ignites hope in your spirit, be determined to make every dream come true. Those negative attributes such as fear, procrastination, dormancy, comparison, depression, suicidal thoughts, loneliness, bitterness, resentment, unforgiveness, and anger are no longer going to be able to thrive in your mental faculties. I pray that every negative attribute applied to you will be permanently evicted from your mind, soul, and spirit.

Hope will now rest. Hope will now rule. Hope will now reside. Let hope be the driving force of your life without end.

I am excited to present to you *Hope Ignited: Stories of Hope by Women for Women.* Let the healing, deliverance, and life-changing journey of hope begin!

Carla Maria Allen
Co-Pastor, Evangelist, Administrator, Teacher
Greater Life Apostolic Church
Detroit, Michigan
www.greaterlifeapostolic.net

INTRODUCTION

Not long before this book went to press, my niece lost her battle with multiple myeloma; or at least, that is what most people say when someone dies of a terminal illness. She didn't lose. She won the victory. My belief is in the scriptures. I Corinthians 15:55 absolutely says the grave has no victory and the death no sting.

I said all of that because I was hoping and believing in her healing. Really hoping. But my desire was shattered into pieces. What happens when your dreams, aspirations, goals, or hopes are deferred? I was praying in the power of the Holy Spirit and was speaking healing into the atmosphere. After all, Jesus said we could do greater things than He did. So, I expected a creative miracle. I matched my faith with hers, she believed. I was on the phone encouraging her, but the truth was she was encouraging me. I have seen many people suffer; however, my niece went through like a powerhouse. Watching her speak with the power of God from her hospital bed countless times for two years while she fought back was so uplifting. She stood on the hope that God would heal. The day she passed, I was joyfully enjoying my grandsons in the middle of the day. It was such a fantastic day until

I got that call. The tears overcame me. They flooded my face. I did not care that I was out in public.

During the preparation for her Celebration of Life, I found myself crying and wanting to hear her laugh. Honestly, I even questioned prayer. I didn't understand why she didn't get her healing on this side. Her faith was enormously high. But here is what I walked away with; her hope was infectious. I watched her praise God with all her might, and I learned that no matter what we face, we have a choice to be happy and full of joy. I can still see in my mind's eye her contagious smile. She kept it even in the darkest moments of despair and unbearable pain. The love of God and her family remained a constant in her life; they gave her the motivation to hope.

So, for you, my sister, be encouraged. God's love is your constant companion. He will never leave you or forsake you. He has placed inside of us everything we need to walk out our life's mission.

As a child, I was raised to pray, read God's word, do what was right, and live a sanctified life for Christ. What I lacked was how to dominate entirely in every part of my life. As a minister of almost three decades, I know how to command my spiritual side. However, there was a time when I just didn't have the wherewithal to be the greatest woman or entrepreneur. I didn't have a master teacher in my life to show me the practical business and soulical (will, intellect, memory, imagination, and emotions) knowledge. After securing coaches to help me in the areas that would make me a well-rounded individual, I began to thrive. I continue to do so. Consequently, I want women worldwide to be empowered in the trichotomous areas of our life: physically, soulical, and in the spirit.

This book came into existence to offer women in all walks of life how to be the most incredible servants their God uniquely designed them to be. We are fearfully and wonderfully made, but *life can life you*. Hope is so important. That is what happened to the entire world. Not one social-economic, age, gender, ethnic, or religious group could escape the pandemic. It *'lifed'* us. It attempted to disrupt the hope of the even greatest optimist.

One of my frequent goals is to give people hope that they can be the person God meant them to be. This book was literally blown into my spirit. One Saturday morning, God whispered in my ear the word hope. I questioned God because I had a guiding word already. My word for 2021 was transformation. It was my deliverance word for the women I came into contact with daily. So I questioned Him and said, you know I have a word, God. He boldly said to give them hope. He continued, "They need the wind blown back into them; they have been deflated." I began to set things in motion with two summits called Hope Ignited. As I concluded the first summit, He returned and told me to publish an anthology with other women called Hope Ignited.

If you could have seen my face at that moment, with my cheeks twisted, thinking, God, are You for real. See, I had just completed my third book in 24 months, only a week prior. My heart was poured into my book, *Powerful: Grow in You & Unlock Your Purpose*. Every obstacle that could rear its ugly head did. My book was set back a few months because my reasonably new computer crashed, losing all its contents not once but twice. My two other computers wouldn't work, my son was hospitalized three times in six weeks, and a fluke medical poisoning incident almost caused someone to harm me. I was simply barely making it, but I kept the faith. For a week, I couldn't even leave my sofa. I continued to pray and complete the job amid my social and emotional depletion. The first week the book launched, I was surprised when the sticker on the Amazon site said Best Seller. Additionally, it was all worth it when I got a phone call and was told that the opening lines of my book alone gave someone hope. They could relate to my limiting thoughts of how my divorce took a toil, but God said I will give you a husband that will love you like I love the church. And in six years of that audible experience with God He did just that. Wow. How amazing? My book offered hope within the very first pages. Even with all that great news, I was tired and wanted a break, but I was obedient to the Lord. I said yes to the Lord. Praise God that I did because the narratives in this book are incredibly hopeful. I know this book will impact the lives of countless women.

The twelve women in this anthology have shared their stories and have been very transparent. I love to analyze things, so when we received the twelve chapters, I got excited. Biblically, the number twelve represents government. My ministry is named Kingdom Influence, so with great humility, we have the blessed opportunity to provide an outline for your authority to be greater by being empowered by God through these personal vignettes.

This book offers encouragement for women experiencing dreadful news, homelessness, barrenness, abusive relationships, self-doubts, singlehood, divorce, work difficulties, family issues, discrimination, inequalities, childhood challenges, drug additions, spiritual powerlessness, limiting beliefs, learning challenges, sexual exploitations, or helplessness. These twelve powerful women hail from America to Asia in all facets of work, but they all have one common denominator – they desire that you have faith. Some are ministers, and some are not; some are coaches, others are not. They are all powerfully filled with hope to give you hope and watch you rise to levels of more tremendous success in your body, soul, and spirit.

As for my niece, she scribed her own eulogy while she lived. What is your life story? What are the significant or even undesirable things about you? What will people say when it's your last day on earth? Before you go any further and read, I was hoping you could do a quick exercise that I have my clients do. I want you to think about your last day (this is not morbid; this is an energizing challenge). What would you like for people to say about you? Be very specific. Write all the things you want to have accomplished and achieved in your body, soul, and spirit realm. Then as you read through this book, take initiation, and start making tiny needlepoint moves to be your most fabulous self. Allow these stories to challenge you and your mindset.

Whether the woman with this book in her hand is what society calls successful or has plenty of issues while discovering herself, this book will minister to all women who choose to let it. I pray that you are reassured as you read. God bless you.

Your Partner in Success,

Brigitte

HOPE. LEGACY. ELEVATE. IMPACT

Hope.

I remember jumping out of bed. The first thought that came to my mind was, "Oh, no, not again," as I felt the wetness on my legs, then on my feet, as I stood in a puddle on the floor. My mind began to race as I was blindly searching and moving through the rooms with no light as I was trying not to wake anyone. It was just dark. I was engulfed with so much darkness for what seemed like forever as I was trying to get to a place where there was light so that I could see what I thought was the loss of another child.

I then realized as I reached the light that the fluid was clear. At that time, I came to an even more confusing realization that my water had just broken.

So, at 4:03 am, I was now questioning myself on what I was supposed to do? It had not fully sunken in, and my next thought was, what did I do? What went wrong? Why did this happen?

Although my water had just broken, anyone would think it

was supposed to be a happy moment where a soon-to-be mom would be excited and ready to go, but I felt fear, a clutching in my heart, and confusion. At that moment, I thought to myself that I needed to call the nurse; I needed to go to the hospital. What did 'I' do? Why am I always in this situation? Is it 'my' fault?

These thoughts were running through my mind because I was only 31 weeks pregnant, and I wasn't prepared. It was a shock because even after all the initial scares throughout my pregnancy, everything had normalized. I was just released from the care of my high-risk doctor. It just didn't add up. I had to be the one to blame. Not only was I in a self-faulting state, but I was also scared. My whole vision was blurred because I had planned out something so perfect. My heart was set on a natural birth with my doula in contact to help me advocate at the hospital, being surrounded by love, and most importantly, bringing my healthy child into an environment of peace.

In the midst of a global pandemic when so much had already been taken away, I was looking forward to these things I assumed I could control. It was my first time getting this far in a pregnancy. As I had been planning and getting along, I had let go of my apprehensions, found the connection, and exhaled. I had *Hope*.

So that night, my entire birth plan and my after-birth plan just went out the window. Nothing was right anymore. Yet, I took a breath, and in the middle of my mental storm, a sense of calm fell over me. I remembered the *Hope*.

Although I was going through some confusion and uncertainty of the situation, not knowing what would happen next, I had to slow down. I had to remember that connection between me, my baby, and God - the faith that could no longer falter. That faith that sparked my *Hope*...through the unknown, there was calm.

Inside that hospital, it was one of the worst times of my life, yet one of the most amazing things was birthed from it. And even though the pain, dismay, and aloneness, I could feel the *Hope* that ignited my faith.

Legacy.

While lying in the hospital as the medical team assigned to me tried to slow my labor and delay the baby's birth so that the immature organs, including his lungs, could be assisted with medication, I kept envisioning the future and how life would change. But not only was I thinking about how life would change but how I needed to change and grow. Through the pain, uncomfortableness, and sleep deprivation, I could only continue to speak to the baby who had been a part of me for seven months and continue to put my faith in God that this was our time and place to meet.

No matter what they did in the hospital to slow labor, it became evident that there was no stopping this baby from coming, and then three days later, he was born. He was a little over 31 weeks, no problems, breathing on his own during a pandemic. He was ready for life. Seeing his fight and his strength only intensified my hunger for growth. To create a place and a human being that he could look up to and see in her actions, purpose, and *legacy* that is never-ending and unstoppable. It was real. He would be able to see, touch, and feel it.

That hope I had felt not long ago turned into will, igniting a fire to show up and go for everything that I wanted in life to create and set a legacy in place to be passed down. I knew the only way I could do that was by being my best self for him, and to be my best self, I had to embrace every part of me, be authentic and show up for him, and everything else that mattered the most in my life.

The *Legacy* truly began when God gave me Mercy. Only a few short months before did I hold my growing belly and ask God to be merciful. To provide me with mercy. I asked my husband during this time to show mercy. Every day of my pregnancy that any doubt crept in, that there was any joy, that light shone, or I felt a little darkness, I asked God for mercy. So he was called Mercy. That was the beginning of the *Legacy*.

So right now, I want to offer a tiny bit of encouragement and advice.

1. What matters most is to be your best self and be your best self which is your authentic self. Be that for you and everybody you have to show up for, for those who need you most.

2. There is someone out in the world waiting on you who needs the gift that only you have for them. Who are you to block their blessing? God has given you a purpose and a gift to share, and once you start to embrace yourself and share your gift honestly, you shall see what you have been waiting for.

3. Look into your mirror and ask yourself how unstoppable am I? What am I afraid of, and is my *Legacy* more powerful than my fear?

I bet you know the answer. Where will your *Legacy* begin?

Elevate

When your mind becomes open to what the universe has for you, you begin to think differently. It sometimes only takes that one life event or circumstance to occur for you to start to realize that you are in control indeed. You control who you are, your actions, your path, thoughts, emotions, and life. You are in control.

It all started with hope for me. It truly began with hope after all that I had experienced, but it grew into something bigger. It hit me that I no longer wanted to hide any parts of me in any particular form. I no longer wished to hold onto or mend relationships that served no real purpose. I only wanted peace and happiness in my life. I wanted to wake, interact, and go to sleep at night without breaking that feeling of peace.

I would say to *Elevate- to improve morally, intellectually, or culturally* begins with you. You would have to focus on and improve yourself. We cannot control or change those around us, but we can change ourselves and become an example for those who come into our path. True influence.

On your path to change, you would need to have a motivator. One thing that you would never give up on. For me, it was every day that I traveled to the hospital and laid my eyes on the baby boy who I knew was a fighter, strong-willed, and determined. I saw a reflection of myself and knew that there was no way I could ever give anything less than my best for him.

What is your #1 Motivator? What or who could you never give up on. If you ever thought about it, you would surely stand up and go even harder for just having that second thought that you wanted to quit. If at this moment you don't have a motivator and you haven't defined your why, do so. Maybe you are feeling some apprehension or fear. It would be best if you didn't feel bad at this moment. I want you to take a step back. Find a moment and place of peace to have a seat and get really open and honest with yourself. I want you to answer these questions.

What's standing in your way? What's stopping you from going all out and unleashing who you are? What are the best parts of you? Who are you that no one else sees? Who are you? What is it that you would like to see change?

Set a date to take action. We are the only ones that can make that change happen. When you start to take action, even imperfect action, you will *Elevate.*

Elevation comes with authenticity- the quality of being genuine or real.

If you are genuine, you have a higher rate of success. You move more naturally, and it comes easier because there's no pretending, there's no extra brainpower, you can show up and be you. You have a vision in sight, and you get there much faster because you are focused on success, not keeping up with the Joneses. You are not worried about fitting in, or who approves, or validation, and you have a legacy to put into place. That is your focus. The only path is your purpose, and along that path, you are spreading your gift.

This doesn't happen overnight, but it happens with practice. Here's how to put it into practice:

Write down three ways that you can practice or put into action, being genuine daily. I want you to commit to at least practicing one of these things for the next seven days. When you reach seven days, I want you to keep going until you're doing it without thinking about it. You want your actions to be so genuine that it becomes a lifestyle, becomes second nature, and you don't have to think about it. Once you make that one a habit, start on the next one. Make sure to start with something that creates the least resistance—the easiest one. So you can set yourself up for success and build a little confidence while doing so. Celebrate yourself for every win.

I promise when you start embracing every part of you, the good, the bad, the ugly, indifferent, your whole you, your life will change. There's no need to hide or shadowban the parts of you that you are unsure if people will accept because nobody's perfect. We're all humans; we're all flawed. We're all imperfectly perfect.

Sometimes, it is easier just to be what someone else wants us to be to play it safe and stay comfortable. If you are okay with being easy and comfortable, I want you to start getting okay with hard and uncomfortable. Take a daily step outside of your comfort zone and get acquainted with courage and confidence. Your light will begin to shine. You will ditch your comfort zone. This is where you *Elevate*.

Impact

To come full circle, you have to see change. You can't finish where you began. I didn't start off knowing that all it would take was a little hope to take me from conception to birth, both figuratively and literally speaking. I never imagined that I would have had the experiences I did or that my circumstances would force me to change my mindset and look deeper at my purpose. Staying up most nights, secluded and isolated from the world with a newborn, I was forced to reevaluate my gifts and recognize that I was playing it all safe. I wasn't showing up or going big enough.

That was my point of elevation. Right now, if you know you are holding anything back, I want to offer you this love and strength as I say these words:

> *I want you to let go of all the inhibitions, stressors, and apprehension, take a big breath, and let it all out. Breathe in again and let it go slowly, exhale. Now, I want you to envision what matters most to you in this world. As you're bringing in that vision, I want you to imagine now what you want your life to be. And as you're envisioning this, I want you to know that the sky is not the limit. I want you to go big. I want you to visualize what you want your life to look like and then go bigger. There are no boundaries. There are no limitations—only everything you can imagine.*

What does that look like for you? Where are you? What do you feel? What does it feel like? What do you see around you? What does it sound like? What does it smell like? Inhale.

What does it taste like? Exhale.

What do you see? Who is there with you? What is that vision? How does it feel? What do you feel like as you're sitting in your limitless vision? I want you to pause and take it in, and I want you to remember this feeling. I want you to use this feeling to move you forward when you want to shrink and not show up as all of who you are. I want you to use it when you doubt who you are absolutely Purposed to be and when you don't believe your gift is good enough. Use it when you get those doubts, and the limiting beliefs creep in.

I want you to sit in this feeling daily. I want you to power up and ignite the flame to push forward with your vision. This is where you will make an *Impact*.

Each day that you work to elevate your mindset and evolve while being open to embracing your absolute best self is a day that you *Impact* your own life and/or the life of others. I wholeheartedly believe that we have to impact our own lives before we can impact anyone else.

We were all put here with a purpose, and the only way to truly walk in it is to accept yourself, open your heart, and open your mind to what that actually is.

Impact is having a substantial effect on someone or something. So once again, I ask you to put it into action. Daily sit in your vision, practice being who you are with all your faults and flaws, imperfectly perfect. It all begins in mind and then extends through your actions.

I want you to envision where your best self can take you, what's out there for you, what's waiting for you. Use your vision to fuel your fire and light that fire under you to keep moving every day, even when you don't want to. Reignite daily. Even when Life happens, I want you to use it to push you forward.

Processing everything that I went through during the pandemic, having the baby eight weeks early, taking him home three weeks before they said he would be released, and then being isolated with no support was not easy. I literally could have just broken down and given up. Everything was not perfect; in fact, it was far from it, but I had that igniter, that motivator. I know you have had your own igniters occur. Prove your circumstances wrong.

Step into your power. I knew that I had to step into my best self and be who I am. I would only walk in my authenticity towards my purpose and what was out there for me to lead and create a legacy for the children depending on me. I concluded that even though I went through the experience of feeling first hope, next fear, and then faith, I couldn't stay in that one place. I had to keep moving. My *Impact* needed to be felt by those who were waiting for my gift.

I want you to do the same. Show up as your best self, first for you and then for everyone who's waiting for your gift because you are not the one that's going to be denying their blessing. You're going to be the one helping them reach their blessing. I want you to know today absolutely you can create your legacy, and all it takes is you. You want to use this person right here. Who doesn't need to change a thing because you are you naturally and perfectly? You just have to let her out. She's waiting to be unleashed. Permit your authentic, best self so that you can go after that vision that's sitting there waiting for you to get there.

You Were Born to Impact. That woman you are inside and out, fighting through *Hope* to create *Legacy*, to *Elevate* her thinking, and Impact her life and the world. We got you.

CAMEASHA MUHAMMAD

Founder of Born to Impact, Cameasha is a Transformation Coach and Behavior Consultant. Her master's degree in forensic psychology helps her serve her clients with incredible results. She enables others through a process to create, plan, and execute their vision authentically, confidently, and on purpose with intentional impact.

For more information, check out her services on:

www.cameasha.com

HOPELESS ROMANTIC

Most girls dream of the fairytale kind of love - that hopeless romantic movie that ends just right. Fireworks, rose petals, and sweet morning messages. Well, this chapter is for you, my sister. It's for the woman who is still hoping for her natural fire to be ignited by the man of her dreams.

Have you found yourself giving up on the idea of the love of your life finding you? Him discovering you as the proverb instructs us that he will. Or maybe you feel like one day you're watching the Lifetime movie channel, and the next day you're starring in one. You are the main character of the not-so-feel-good movie. Because honestly, you're completely over the dating scene.

My name is Maria Green, and I am a living testimony to what it means to ignite hope during hopeless situations. I am the girl who's always smiling, always eager to encourage others, yet I found myself feeling hopeless, yearning for more even with the smile on my face.

Everyone has the moment where they question their situation with a why. What's the rationale? But after your mind starts questioning and asking why it happened, please ask yourself this question, What can I do now? Don't stop at your why because where you are going is more significant than the why of your past.

I can vividly remember being in my hopeless moment; as tears began to fall down my face, God stopped me and said, wipe your tears and thank me. I was slightly taken back by the stern sound in his voice towards me. His response wasn't cradling my little emotional rant. It was a moment of full correction for his intent to switch my direction for my life. It was as if he was telling me I was being a brat for him protecting me from something that was purposed to destroy me. At that very moment, my hope was ignited. I could really see it. I understood.

I dried my face and said, okay, God, it's you and me. I was ready to spend every moment with God. I found myself planning actual date nights with Jesus. I can remember the aroma-filled room as I was popping my popcorn, getting dressed up, and grabbing my bible on a Friday evening to sit in my bedroom to talk to Jesus as if he was physically sitting right next to me. He was the best first date ever. That night He showed me my heart, He showed me my help, He showed me my hope. He was preparing me for the Christ-centered courtship romance that would be coming sooner than I could have ever imagined.

It was a wake-up call; I was not seeking 'anything' but Jesus. I wasn't seeking 'anyone' but Jesus. My hope was in Jesus, I ditched the hopeless romantic chick flicks, and I sought Jesus. I stopped strolling social media, and I strolled my bible. I chased his heart as He was well equipped to handle mine—what an awakening.

He opened the doors of my heart, but it only was because I decided to let him in. Sis, is He knocking?

Is Jesus knocking on your door, but you have Him locked out? Is his seat filled with a counterfeit relationship? How can he fill a seat that's already full? Sis is it time to reignite your relationship with Jesus. I am here to encourage you to find hope in your relationship with Jesus and trust Him to place His best in your life. I encourage you to use my three-step strategy to find HOPE in your future romantic relationship.

Step One
Make Ministry your priority. Get to work for Jesus, stop missing church intentionally, and forgetting to spend time with Jesus.

Step Two
Embrace the wait, embrace it because it could be closer than it appears.

Step Three
Through faith, keep hope in your heart. Even when you don't see it, see it!

The bible says, "Now faith is the substance of things hoped for, the evidence of things not seen."

Therefore, my sisters, you have to see yourself in a holy, healthy, happy relationship before you see it. Allow God's timing to catch up with your faith. I am here in this chapter to tell you that authentic, valid, Godly marriages exist. I am married to the most amazing husband, and it's only because of the Hope that God ignited in me. God told me NO to other relationships, and it was a plan in the process.

Trust God's process. Trust God's NO, and His YES will be worth the wait. May your heart be filled with the fire you need to love on Jesus while He finds you your heart's desire.

MARIA GREEN

Maria Green is a proud principal and consummate results-driven educator. She loves children and serving the people of God. Her role as an Evangelist allows her to minister to people, especially women. Her energy is infectious. She lives in Michigan, happily married with two children.

My great hope is to laugh as much as I cry; to get my work done and try to love somebody and have the courage to accept the love in return.

- **Maya Angelou**

PRAISING YOUR WAY THROUGH

Psalm 34:1-4
I will bless the LORD at all times: his praise shall continually be in my mouth. My soul shall make her boast in the LORD: the humble shall hear thereof, and be glad. O magnify the LORD with me, and let us exalt his name together. I sought the LORD, and he heard me, and delivered me from all my fears.

Every morning I wake up and pray, commanding my day in the Lord. Typically, throughout the course of the day, we don't really give God praise as we should. But we give honor to earthly things that we can see. I'm so guilty of this because the bible tells us to walk by faith and not by sight. The emotional, nurturing, and caring side of a woman reacts to situations before allowing the Lord to handle them.

I remember praying for a situation, and I allowed my emotions (Flesh) to try and fix the problem, but it made everything worse. I asked the Lord to fix the situation again. As clear as someone speaking directly to me, I heard the Lord say, "Move out the way!" It scared me because I heard but didn't see anyone. So, I changed my prayer to "Lord, move me out the way so you can fix this situation." I never prayed for that situation again. When you realize who is fighting for you, you can rest assured that victory belongs to you.

That's why it's so important to give God praise because it confuses the devil. When we dwell on situations, sickness, shortcomings, we allow the enemy room to allow our imagination to run wild. We start thinking of the worst that could happen. That's how fear, depression, and anxiety creep in our minds, and we can't see what God is doing because the enemy's scare tactics blind us.

So, when we praise God, it serves the enemy notice that we are not scared and that God has all Power over the enemy.

When the enemy tries to remind you of your past, you just tell him, "I'm an Overcomer." When the enemy tries to tell you that Jesus doesn't love you, you tell him, "Can't nobody do me like Jesus." When the enemy tries to tell you that you will never be anything, you tell him, "I'm a child of the King." When the enemy tries to tell you, you will never get out of your situation; you tell him, "Jesus will work it out."

When we praise God, we celebrate God for what he has already done in our lives and what he is currently doing.

In everything give thanks; for this is the will of God in Christ Jesus for you. (1 Thessalonians 5:18 NKJV)

We must give thanks in all things. Just like a person provides you with something, you would reply by saying, "Thank you." That's common courtesy and respect. Therefore, if we can thank a person for something other than life, I'm sure we can thank God every day, hour, minute, and second for allowing His only son (Jesus) to die so that we may have life. Wow, that statement alone in itself is enough to shout to the rooftop… THANK YOU, JESUS!

I grew up in church watching people praising God and thought to myself, do they do this other than at church. Do you see people walking in the mall with their hands raised, giving thanks unto God? Do you see people riding the city bus singing praises unto God? Do you see people in the grocery store sharing the love of God with others? Why do we wait until Sunday to give God praise?

I went on a missionary trip to Spain a few years ago. It was a trip where we ministered to young ladies caught up in human trafficking. The church that invited us had service every night we were there. The first night of service, I noticed only about two cars in the parking lot. I thought to myself, wow, nobody came to service tonight. To my surprise, the church was filled with over 300 people. They all walked to service far and near.

The young ladies who were caught up in human trafficking were in service that night. It was so hard to identify them because everybody was engaged in worship. It was a beautiful thing to see everyone on one accord.

During a particular time, the young ladies had to leave to prepare for the streets. After service, I begged the church administrators to take us where the young ladies were at. They responded by letting us know that it was very dangerous. Nevertheless, we were able to ride down the longest street I have ever seen. Young ladies were everywhere waiting on a pickup.

I'm sharing this story with you because regardless of where you are in your situation, God will meet you where you are at. Those young ladies praised and worshipped God as I had never seen before. They wrote down their prayer request on a piece of paper and gave it to us. As I read the request to myself, I was in tears because it was the dollar amount of their bounty for their freedom. I thought about many situations we pray for and how we want tangible things. Those young ladies were praising God for freedom – liberty from sexual exploitation.

Once we arrived back home in Michigan, we learned that a few girls were released because they were not making any money. To God be the glory. I'm sure those Johns saw the God in those young ladies and had to back up. You just don't get released from human trafficking, and you pay your debt. But God has a funny way of doing things. They were released by the blood of Jesus and they praised God.

That's how we confuse the enemy, and that's how we get God's attention. Although those women were in the worst situation anyone could be in as a woman, they still worshipped God because they knew He was the answer to their prayer.

[15] He said: "Listen, King Jehoshaphat and all who live in Judah and Jerusalem! This is what the LORD says to you: 'Do not be afraid or discouraged because of this vast army. For the battle is not yours, but God's. [16] Tomorrow march down against them. They will be climbing up by the Pass of Ziz, and you will find them at the end of the gorge in the Desert of Jeruel. [17] You will not have to fight this battle. Take up your positions; stand firm and see the deliverance the LORD will give you, Judah and Jerusalem. Do not be afraid; do not be discouraged. Go out to face them tomorrow, and the LORD will be with you.'"[18] Jehoshaphat bowed down with his face to the ground, and all the people of Judah and Jerusalem fell down in worship before the LORD. [19] Then some Levites from the Kohathites and Korahites stood up and praised the LORD, the

God of Israel, with a very loud voice.[20] Early in the morning they left for the Desert of Tekoa. As they set out, Jehoshaphat stood and said, "Listen to me, Judah and people of Jerusalem! Have faith in the LORD your God and you will be upheld; have faith in his prophets and you will be successful." [21] After consulting the people, Jehoshaphat appointed men to sing to the LORD and to praise him for the splendor of his[a] holiness as they went out at the head of the army, saying: "Give thanks to the LORD, for his love endures forever."[22] As they began to sing and praise, the LORD set ambushes against the men of Ammon and Moab and Mount Seir who were invading Judah, and they were defeated.
2 Chronicles 20:15-22

Regardless of what you are going through, just know the battle is already won. I look at every storm that I go through in my life as a *Storm of Correction or a Storm of Perfection.*

Have you ever been in a situation where you have prayed about something, and timing was a major factor? You decided to take matters into your own hands, thinking option B would be the answer. So, you continued to pray for the situation over and over until the due date or expiration date was getting closer and closer. For example, you were praying about a relationship, friendship, or marriage that you needed to see a change in the other person asap. So, while you are praying, the person displays no changes at all. You begin to get angry because you need to see some change before throwing in the towel. We are missing in this situation because we need to ask God to work on us (ME). This is where God wants us (ME) to correct some things within (ME). Once God works on ME, others can see the love of God through ME.

The storm of Perfection is where God takes us through some difficult times to strengthen, develop, and perfect a gift to be utilized for his Glory. I remember my husband telling me about a young man who was very good-looking, nicely built, had a lot going for himself, but God spoke to him and told the young man, "I need you to give up everything." Of course, one would think twice about what they heard and who they heard it from. Well, the young man gave up everything and went homeless. He was sleeping on the ground, the streets and benches begging for money and food. He said to God after a few weeks, "Ok, God, I did it." God said, "You haven't really BECAME homeless." God told him He needed for him to BECOME 100% homeless. Put himself in their shoes. The young man mentally became homeless. His hair grew out, wearing the same clothes every day, eating out of the garbage, smelling bad, and feeling rejection. The young man stated homeless for over a year. He started ministering to the homeless. God started using him in the homeless community until he brought the homeless to churches to be baptized. To his surprise, the churches rejected the homeless people. That rejection opened his eyes to see what the church must BECOME to help those in need.

Jehoshaphat was a willing vessel that God used. God gave him specific instructions to follow, and if Jehoshaphat followed those instructions, he would not have had to fight the battle. Jehoshaphat and his army song praise to God. The next thing they knew, the battle was won. Again, Praises confuse the enemy.

Regardless of the storm, you have the VICTORY! Never doubt. Continue to keep faith and watch God move in your situation. We must see how God sees it. We must talk like God. We must walk like God. We must think like God.

Never allow the enemy to give you negative thoughts. If so, you will find yourself speaking negative things like, my sinus are bothering me; my leg hurts, I feel like I'm coming down with a cold. Those are all negative words. God said by His stripes we were Healed. So are we going to stand on His word or believe a lie from the devil?

We must walk in Power and speak with Authority!

Jehoshaphat never doubted. He stood firm on what God had done for them. He proclaimed the word of the Lord. He spoke with Authority and followed the command of the Lord.

That's BOLDNESS.

You need to have that same BOLDNESS when the enemy tries to throw you a curveball. You stand on the word of God and use what God has already said.

"Lord, YOU said by Your stripes I'm healed. Lord YOU said when praises go up, blessings come down. Lord, YOU said You will never leave me nor forsake me."

Now serve notice to the devil! I need you to say, "Satan, I command you. Go and leave God's people alone." You have the power and authority because you are a child of the King. According to Psalm 22:3, God inhabits (live in or occupy) the praises of His people.

I can recall hearing about the pandemic and how the news kept talking about it all day. The goal was to put fear in the minds of those watching until it turned into anxiety. I stop watching the news. I began to sing praises throughout the day. I began to pray throughout the day. I began to read the bible throughout the day. So that confused the enemy because how can one rejoice during a pandemic? I refused to allow this pandemic to bring depression and anxiety, so I created an atmosphere of praise that I carried wherever I went.

When you allow the Holy Spirit to take complete control of your life, you can walk into a room and change the entire atmosphere. Therefore, don't allow what you see and hear to control your day. When we honor God, He lives and resides in the place where He is being honored.

So, this pandemic didn't change me; I changed the pandemic to a *prayerdemic* where I began to pray for the things I saw and heard— petitioning God to turn situations around. I didn't dwell upon the negative. I began to turn the negative into positive thoughts. The Bible tells us to think about good things. That's precisely what I did; I began to turn phone conversations around. When negative conversations on my job appeared, I intercepted them with positive thoughts or prayer. We must watch what we speak in the atmosphere. The enemy is looking for an open door that would allow him to use your negative thoughts to attack your mind. Always talk about life, positive things, and good things from above. Just like the enemy is waiting for an open door, God is waiting for someone to speak life into a dead situation so He can dispatch his angels to bring forth His word. Just know that God is with you.

There's nothing too hard for God. When your back is up against the wall, praise your way through because VICTORY is just around the corner.

MICHELLE ROBINSON

First Lady Michelle Robinson is from Jacksonville, Florida but resides in Ypsilanti, Michigan. She is a mighty prophetic woman of God, talented songstress, anointed worshipper, and powerful prayer warrior. Her heart cries out for people. She works alongside her husband Pastor Michael Robinson at Ypsilanti Community Church to help transform lives through experiences of signs, wonders, and miracles.

To not have any hope is where things start to get really bleak. Things are possible. The impossible can be possible.

Sarah Paulson

HOPE NOT FEARS: A LIFE OF JOY

May your choices reflect your hopes, not your fears.
~Nelson Mandela

Ever feel like you're drowning in your life? Were you overwhelmed by the needs of everyone around you? Parents, siblings, spouse, in-laws, kids, friends, boss, coworkers, government. Just one need or expectation after another pulling on your time, energy, and last few nerves. I've felt that a few times in my life. Hate to admit it, but it'll likely happen a few more times as I make my way through life. But I'm not here to remind you of all that feels like an obligation or burden in your life. I want to remind you that a life of joy is possible if you learn to choose your pain.

Sounds counterintuitive, I know, but let me tell you a story to try to explain what I mean. In 2015, I was at yet another low in my lifetime. I had left my husband and stepkids in 2013 and moved back to Singapore with my toddler to start over. My family was here – my mother, youngest brother, grandparents, aunts, cousins. Singapore had the largest concentration of blood relatives globally, so I thought this would be the best place for me to feel supported as I turned a new leaf. Leaving was the most challenging choice I'd ever made to date because it's not quite like trying to move on after someone passes away. There was grief over choosing to leave people behind who were still very much alive and trying to understand my worth against what felt like not being or doing enough to be a priority to them. Depression with a two-year-old was not fun. There were days when I couldn't get out of bed or stop crying, but my daughter still needed to eat, play, and share, so I was grateful for having family around, for the first time in 8 years, who could step in for me so she wouldn't miss anything.

Gradually I pulled myself together and began to reestablish my self-worth. I became a more active parent; I homeschooled her, went on adventures, played, laughed, and spent time with family. Eventually, my family stepped in and said, "You need to get a job. You've been lounging long enough." So, I did. I found an event planning job and learned to manage the time between corporate life and a single parent. I was no longer a burden financially to my family. Soon after that, my family stepped in again and said, "It's not fair to expect your mother to care for your child while you are working. You need to find childcare." I obliged and weighed the option of day care or, as is the custom in Singapore, hiring a live-in nanny. I was not too fond of the idea of having someone outside the family raising my daughter because I didn't trust that they would care for her the way family would. The alternative was to have an outsider live with me and help me raise my child. Not feeling like I had much choice, I opted for the nanny so that my daughter could still spend time with family but was not a burden to them.

Around the same time, my work life was becoming chaotic. My boss, despite being married, was of the impression that hiring women on his team entitled him to unbecoming behavior, and I was trying my best to avoid unnecessary altercations. My avoiding him led him to panic, and he began documenting anything that would justify termination. The other women in the office were flattered by his advances, but I was highly uncomfortable. There were many conversations from friends and family attempting to convince me not to quit, not take him personally, assuring me he was quite harmless, that men are just like that here. Still, I couldn't shake the feeling of never wanting to be in a position where I felt obligated due to favor. Eventually, as I expected, he let me go, and I was back to square one looking for work. Unfortunately, the minute I told my family that I was let go after six months, each of them, in their own way, showed their disappointment in my not being able to hold a job for longer and began to question my ability to be a team player. Their advice was just to go along to get along to establish financial stability.

An uncle called in a "favor" so that I didn't go too long without work, and I found myself back in hospitality. I've always loved the variety of interactions you get from work in hospitality, and I felt better that this company was a global brand. I figured that HR would be there to intervene if anyone got any ideas, and other than that, a big company meant rules and regulations and a chain of command which was a massive departure from my last job with one boss and a team of six. With the helper in place living with me and my family and a job I felt I could trust, I started back at the bottom of the ladder, ready to climb. This job was shift work, so it took a little doing to get my body to acclimate, and I had to work to find spaces of time where I could still homeschool my daughter. I was determined not to become dependent on the systems I had in place to take care of her so much that I lost touch as a parent. Depending on my schedule, I would teach the before or after my shift, and we soon found a rhythm that worked well.

Work was exciting, and my previous experience with hotels and spas was a blessing to me. Orientation took about three months as I worked through the various departments to learn how the hotel communicated to provide the best possible guest experience. It was, after all, a 5-star hotel, and I was working for the VIP Guest team. As much as there are rules and protocols at work, they still expect you to bring something personal and extra to each guest's experience. Good experiences meant social media reviews, and guests were encouraged to name employees who made a difference in their stay. I love connecting with people, and my various travels have taught me that people are only strangers for a few moments. Hospitality was the perfect way to use my listening skills to help guests feel extra special and taken care of. I would use whatever resources I had available to create small meaningful gestures and did my best to avoid cliché extras like the token extra hotel amenities.

I took great pride in this skill set. When asked what I did to deserve a review, I boldly let my team know, anything from remembering birthdays or life milestones was commemorated by creating mini-posters or handmade cards and similar crafts. But that's where the issues began. Since I was going above and beyond a regular employee's initiative, people began to find fault with my approach to my work. Little things like waiting until someone relieved me of my shift so I could eat instead of leaving on time became a cause for complaint, and slowly they began to limit my abilities to do my job well. Eventually, they even began chastising me for the way I wore my makeup or hair.

Working shifts had me stretched thin because my shift never ended on time. I was doing my best to show up for my daughter in the spaces of time I had between my work schedule, but I felt like I was failing her. I felt like I was missing a lot of "firsts" and often felt terrible about other people raising her on my behalf while I was out "making a living." I wanted desperately to get to a place where people would stop judging me and make decisions simply because I felt competent and not out of obligation to follow advice. I knew my elders had succeeded in life by following the crowd, but I had a nagging feeling that there had to be a better way than to miss my daughter's childhood while trading hours for money just to live hand to mouth, pay bills and repeat.

There is a limit for anyone's tolerance, and I was all for compliance, but I began to act out when the criticism started to border on petty. I didn't see how the way I looked affected my ability to care for the guests and realized that I was mistaken for a few other employees because we all looked similar – uniform, hair length, duty location. To ensure my guests knew who I was, I cut all my hair off and reduced my makeup to a more natural look, so I stood out. This again aggravated an already sensitive team, and in the end, I chose to leave a good job because I felt so restricted and unappreciated. Even this choice for my mental health had an adverse reaction at home. Once again, I was lectured on the need for a mother to provide for her child adequately, and my "rebellion" for quitting another job was unforgivable. I had thrown my uncle's "favor" away, and it was perceived as disrespect to his sticking his neck out for me. It was around this same time that my grandmother passed away, and my grandfather fell ill. Everyone was concerned about whether I would be able to help out or whether I would become a burden to my family.

Pressured, I once again put myself out there, looking for work, and ended up creating a curriculum for the pre-school crowd. I thoroughly loved this because it fell in line with my homeschooling beliefs - use everyday items to help teach, make lessons hands-on as much as possible and allow the child's imaginations to guide them towards solutions. Around the same time, my grandfather passed away, so we had moved to my mother's house. Soon after the funeral, my mother left the country as it was too difficult for her; after losing both parents suddenly. I was home alone with my nanny and toddler. I would go to work at least safe in the knowledge that I had someone at home to take care of my baby girl, and she didn't have to be in school just yet. I wanted to hold off putting her into the school system to enjoy her carefree childhood a little longer. But that was short-lived. One day, my baby girl, highly embarrassed, confessed that our nanny had left her on the playground by herself and she had needed to go to the bathroom but ended up going outside in a corner somewhere. Enraged, I decided not to take further chances on my daughter's well-being and quickly arranged to remove our nanny from our lives. Suddenly I had to figure out how to care for my daughter while I was at work. I found a daycare close to my office and enrolled her as quickly as possible.

Raising my daughter without a nanny was highly frowned upon, and my relatives advised that I replace rather than remove the nanny altogether. I didn't think I could go through the growing pains of training a new nanny, much less trust anyone who wasn't family with my daughter's well-being. I just put their expectations and opinions and my fear of being judged aside and worked on a solution I could live with. I faced my greatest fear, living in a country without help to raise my daughter, and was determined to make it work somehow. I created a curriculum for drama and Science during the day and managed the house by night. There was finally a rhythm and peace to our lives. I could test my curriculum on my daughter, and I alone was responsible for how she was raised outside of school. This worked for a while, but a simple complaint about a song choice at work led to panic, and eventually, they let me go rather than work out a solution.

So, it was on to the next gig. This time I found myself working as a marketer for a tuition service. They hired me as a favor to my uncle (again), intending to use my style of community building and my experience overseas to entice parents to choose them over the competition. They were even flexible with me about my daughter. By this time, my daughter was enrolled in public school and the school day started at 7:30 am and ended at 1:45 pm. I was allowed to come in early and leave at lunch to pick her up and continue my day until we closed the center at 7 pm. They loved everything on my resume, and at first, it was about getting to know their culture, documenting their processes, and taking pictures to help promote their services. Ultimately, their fears took over, and rather than trust my experience in social media, and they were adamant about me changing to sound more like the locals and using tried and true (and outdated) strategies like print ads and flyers. Even when they ventured towards Facebook Ads and open houses, they led with their fears, and when sounding like a local failed, they blamed me and let me go. Needless to say, this confirmed my uncle's suspicions that, once again, I was not a team player and was generally difficult to manage. There I was back at square one: unemployed, with a kid in school, and judged for my 'inefficiencies.'

My family was slowly distancing themselves from me, and it felt like I was losing respect from them. I was beginning to feel like a failure both at work and home because it didn't seem like anyone believed I could provide adequately for my daughter.

A colleague who witnessed firsthand how hard I had worked at the tuition center and how difficult the work environment had been suggested that I join him in an independent project. He was helping a group establish an international school, and he thought I'd be a great fit to manage the project. We started from the ground up, from choosing the location, planning the layout of classrooms, managing the build-out, to furnishing and decorating. I built relationships with local contractors, created and managed our social media presence, and even populated our blog to always be in the top 5 search results on Google. I was happily employed and thriving until the investors stepped in and were no longer silent partners. We went from gaining exposure and attracting word-of-mouth interest to barely any inquiries. My blog articles were pulled because they felt they were too confusing, and they chose to go after parents who were leaving another school versus keeping to the international school concept. Not only was work becoming more chaotic, but their inability to respect work hours was beginning to affect my home life as well. Constantly held up with last-minute requests, I was perpetually late to pick up my daughter, who was now enrolled in after-school care. The student care center closed promptly at 7 pm, and there were many nights when I ran from the bus stop while on the phone with the center, desperately trying to reach my daughter on time. My being adamant about leaving work on time coupled with their various marketing failures were once again chalked up to my not being enough of a team player. They continued to require more of my time, and I did the best I could to accommodate. At my wit's end, I became increasingly afraid for my financial stability and doing my very best not to be dismissed from yet another job.

I come from a chaotic childhood, and I can more than handle stress from the world around me. I always managed to keep adjusting to do what I had to. But when life begins to affect my child, I have to put my foot down. At this point, the baby girl would wake up at 6:30 am; we'd leave to drop her at school by 7:00 am. I'd head to work from school and rush to pick her up by 7:00 pm. We'd walk home, check over her homework, eat dinner, and it would be time for her to sleep by 8:30 pm. I was expected to work weekends because that was the best time to host open houses to attract new students to the school. It was maddening, and I felt like I barely saw my daughter. I found myself looking back over my life in the last few years.

I am capable of working hard. I'm a workaholic and often eat at my desk or just work through lunch when I'm on shift. I did my very best to accommodate everyone's opinions and beliefs about what success looked like and always seemed to come up short. Every decision so far had been out of fear. Fear of not making money. Fear of being a burden. Fear of not being respected by my family. Fear of not being recognized for my work. Fear of being hated by my daughter for not being around.

ENOUGH

I distinctly remember the day I decided to hand in my resignation at the international school. It was another weekend work event that I had dragged my daughter to. I was tired of compromising. I no longer wanted my name to be associated with anything to do with their marketing. I was looking at this sweet face as we stole 15 minutes to have lunch and decided that I wanted to build a new life on our terms. A life where we had time to play, study, enjoy the sunshine or the rain… really live. For the first time, I quit without a backup plan. Without savings. Without support. I had the current month's paycheck in hand and decided to take a chance. I removed the stress of a toxic work environment. I chose not to tell my family that I quit so I could mute the lectures that would follow and block the pressure to get a conventional "job." I chose to put my daughter first and build a life around what would help create an environment for her to thrive truly! That was five years ago.

I made a decision based on hope. The hope that a 9-5 wasn't the only way to make money. The hope that rushing through life could be avoided. The hope that I was enough to raise a healthy, happy child. It wasn't without some rock-bottom struggles, but suddenly, without all the voices, opinions, expectations, rules, regulations, I was free to follow my heart and create a life that fit our specific needs. It's a simple life without frills. We make our own schedule outside of school hours. I work around her sleep habits. We are happy and peaceful. I am proof that 'theirs' is not the only way to live and succeed. If you are brave enough to distance yourself from things and people that cause panic, anxiety, depression, anger, you make space for yourself to listen to your own heart. To actually hear what your soul craves and how to define happiness for you personally. Based on hope instead of fear, I decided I had become steady enough to reach back and help others because I no longer need rescuing. I made a decision in faith (based on hope); it has opened my life up to so many possibilities I'd never even considered before. The fear had me continuously reducing myself to fit into someone else's definition of love, happiness, and success. Hope allowed me to define it all for myself. I made a decision based on hope, and it has made all the difference.

RASATHI RASIAH

Rasathi Rasiah is an International Coach and Speaker who specializes in teaching trauma-informed emotional intelligence. She believes that while we all understand and feel the same emotions, the reason those emotions surface is specific to our individual life experiences. Emotional Intelligence is the key to improving all your relationships – familial, platonic, romantic, and business. Her mission is to teach skills that can be used in every situation that involves human interaction regardless of age, gender, race, or culture. Owner of the brand Rasath1, Rasathi is very active on social media and hosts the Night Owl Podcast. She can be followed on YouTube.

Hope is the thing with feathers that perches in the soul - and sings the tunes without the words - and never stops at all. – Emily Dickerson

TO HAVE FAITH

"To have faith is to be sure of the things we hope for, to be certain of the things we cannot see" -Hebrews 11:1 (GNT)

Faith is a vital tool in our lives. It is the gas needed to be able to drive the car. It is the key that opens the door to your home. The thing that takes a dream and makes it into a reality. There are times when we are faced with hard issues and situations that become mountains, and our faith is needed for us to rise to the occasion. Our faith is the force that moves the mountain of hardships out of the way.

Three years ago, I was faced with a complicated situation of what seemed like a mountain standing in front of me. I became pregnant with my second child, and one particular day I was headed to my prenatal appointment at the doctor's office. I was so excited to hear the heartbeat on the ultrasound while I lay back and relax as the warm ultrasound gel was gently placed on my stomach and the doppler moved around. Only a few minutes into the doctor's entrance, I started to see the concern as he just continued to move the doppler around on my stomach. There was nothing but silence. Something didn't seem right, I thought. He looked up and began to talk.

"I can't find the baby's heartbeat," he said.

As he continued, he told me that the baby was showing no signs of breathing and that I should be experiencing a miscarriage within the next week. If that didn't happen, they could perform a procedure to remove the baby, but my body should naturally have a miscarriage in a few days.

The unexpected news stabbed me in the heart like a knife, and the room fell silent. *To have faith is to be sure of the things we hope for, to be certain of the things we cannot see.* These words went across my mind like a banner, and something rose up in me.

"I will see you at my appointment next week," I said.

He looked at me with a shocked expression on his face, and I scheduled my appointment for that next week. Walking out the door, I knew Faith was on the scene at that moment and that the baby I was carrying was, in fact, alive and not dead. I got in the car and immediately called my husband. We got in agreement, and he started to pray with me on the phone. Once I got off the phone, I knew I needed to go straight home. I needed to make sure that I allowed nothing to distract me from what I believed and stood on. I knew that if I went to do all the errands I had to run and all the things that I needed to complete on my agenda, I would have started to think about what the doctor said, not what God said about the situation. I needed to go straight home. I needed to go pray and see what God said in this situation.

Often, if something goes wrong or something terrible happens, we can immediately think that we need to call and talk to a friend, family member, check google, do research, etc. I knew that I had to stand on bold faith. I could not ALLOW even a tiny bit of doubt to come into my mind. As a wife and being one with my husband, I spoke to him about it, and we both had faith and went into prayer. We didn't tell anyone about it or what was going on, which was CRUCIAL. Bold faith is sometimes doing what seems impossible. It's going against the natural standard and bringing the supernatural and all of heaven into the picture. People's opinions and what they think doesn't matter, but God's does!

That day at home, I opened my bible to find a scripture that pertained to what I was going through. I knew that if I spoke God's word into a situation, the problem (mountain) I was faced with would be removed. God's word has the power to manifest itself, so I found Psalm 118:17. *"I will live and not die and proclaim the works of the Lord."* I began to make this scripture more personal to my situation, **"This baby will live and not die and proclaim the works of the Lord!"**

I wrote this down and placed this all over our home. Everywhere I could think of that I would be - in the bedroom, the kitchen, the car, and the living room. This included on the bathroom right in front of the toilet and on the mirror. I could not for a second let any negative thoughts come into my mind. I could speak this scripture over and over and over.

As I walked into my follow-up appointment with my husband the next week, I felt at peace. Extreme peace. I didn't need the doctor to confirm for me to believe because I knew already that this baby would live and not die and proclaim the works of the Lord. When the doppler slid across on my stomach, without a doubt, I knew I would hear a strong heartbeat. There it was:

whirlll, swhorlll, whirlll, swhorlll whirlll, swhorlll, whirlll, swhorlll

That incredible high pitch melodiously sounded through the speakers of the ultrasound machine. The doctor was shocked; I wasn't. I smiled because God's Word came to life, and what seemed impossible was made possible with God. Thank you, God!

This was just the beginning. What the devil thought he could destroy was blessed and made ten times greater. I used the same scripture for my subsequent pregnancy. I was able to help other women who were struggling to have kids, who suffered multiple miscarriages, and who were having rough pregnancies. God used me to pray with them and speak Psalms 118:17. I find great joy to say that these women are now mothers who not only have one but multiple, healthy children.

TIFFANY SAUNDERS

Tiffany Saunders graduated from Eastern Michigan University. Shortly after graduating, she answered the call to ministry. For over a decade Tiffany has walked in her calling bringing transformation and prophetic counsel to people of all ages. God uses her in the supernatural realm. Additionally, she is a wife, mother, and life coach. She believes her family is her first ministry. Her mantra is, God can do great things through you but getting your house in order is priority.

You may not always have a comfortable life and you will not always be able to solve all of the world's problems at once but don't ever underestimate the importance you can have because history has shown us that courage can be contagious and hope can take on a life of its own.

-Michelle Obama

BECOMING US

Not Just a Pretty Face

For as long as I can remember, I was a good version of myself. Even when I believed I didn't have courage, I was still the best version of myself for that time. As a child, I struggled with thoughts of inadequacies. All I could believe was that I was merely a pretty face. My struggles in school made me think I was worthless. I never understood the deep inner beauty and power within. While I now know that that was not true, the determination and confidence should have been more vital; something was holding me like an anchor to a ship. It was not external, though; it was myself weighing me down. That was until I answered the clarion call to save myself.

My mentor once said to me, "No one is going to save you, Cookie." Those words pierced my soul like a knife cutting raw meat. Could this be true? Was I my 'own' savior of my own destiny? Yes, I was. There is no doubt that God is my Creator and Savior, but here in the physical body, my mantra is if it is going to be, it is up to me.

This epiphany came one day as I heard God say, "Now you're

ready!" I was on a journey of self-discovery and empowerment. It was painful, challenging, and there were many days and nights of hopelessness, but I don't regret those lessons at all. That process shaped me into being an incredible mother, compassionate grandmother, and phenomenal life coach. I enjoyed teaching others about Shadow Work. But don't let me get off-topic. Stay with me, and we'll come to the Shadow Work later in the chapter.

One of the most hurtful times of my life opened me up to be the lifeboat I needed. I would have to be a part of my rescue team. God would help; however, He helps in areas I can't. My job is to assist with the abilities He gave me.

Thirty-plus years of marriage ended, just like that. One day I finally got the courage to walk away. I was able to step into my power but also walk away from what was not serving me. The emotional poison was killing me. Please don't think I am condoning or teaching the practice of divorce. Vows are sacred. But when you get into an unhealthy relationship at 15 and marry at 20 to the mirror image of your abusive parent, that is not a good recipe. As women, we can never tolerate abuse.

I have forgiven my ex-husband. I had to. It was vital to my being. As I did work on myself, I had more compassion and love. My muscles of care and concern were being shaped and formed as if I were a world-class bodybuilder. It is not going to serve me or you to detail the wrong that was acted upon me. So, I will give you an overview. My divorce was finalized after 44 years of officially being married. I had justified my reasons not to leave or complete it earlier. But when

God spoke and said, now you are ready to take responsibility for your life, I had to act and act quickly.

For so many years, I hated my former husband, but it was only the reflection of myself I was hating. His presence in my life made me see the Rochelle I didn't like. It made me visualize the hurtful mirror image of my trauma, but at the same time, his ingenuity and savviness made me trust in my financial stability. Because school was challenging for me, I went into the workforce instead of going to college. I was hooked; I needed the security blanket he offered. That was until the journey to forgive me for all those erroneous decisions. I started forgiving him, dealing with my apprehensions and limiting beliefs that were seared into my psyche as a child.

I had an abusive father and quiet mother who lacked the courage to stand up for herself. While we fared well in life, emotional security was less to be desired. My mother's lessons of love were not the best examples to emulate, but, in all honesty, she did the best she could with what she had. I had to learn to forgive her, my father, and myself as well. My biggest challenge was to stop transferring that into my present and future life. I had to work on being a better best version of myself. Do the work, I told myself. Without self-awareness, forgiveness, and putting that dreaded work in, I couldn't show up as who I authentically was meant to be. It was dreadful. Change does not come easy, especially when you spend decades fighting the process. I didn't want any residual effects of my childhood or marriage traumas to command the rest of my life. I stood up for myself.

It is so beautiful to say today that I show up as a bolder, more confident, determined woman with the hope that those words God said, "the time is now," continue to embolden me. Whenever I am challenged, I remember I may be a work in progress – a diamond in the rough, but I can do everything I set my mind to overcoming. Shadow Work and the rearing of children and their reciprocal love continued to sharpen and develop me.

At the start of my coaching journey, I had a contagious hope for the first time in my life. Now I offer that hope to others. No matter what it looks like, you, my friend, can get over it. I went from the townhouse lifestyle to taking food from stores to feed my girls (I did make amends for the wrong to others during that time). I owned my issues, and I took responsibility for my actions.

I didn't want to suffer financially, so I settled. My lifestyle had been wrapped around living a life that others would think was "the good life." But it was far from that. It was hurting my children, so I got the fortitude and courage to walk away. I put my life in God's hands and began to seek help and support.

After receiving coaching and becoming a certified coach, I was able to walk out a different scenario. My hope was ignited. I was better for it. Even my only granddaughter is better for it today. She is a confident and driven 'Cookie.'

I was not perfect, but I was the ideal person to help save myself.

Segregated

That is not the word you typically hear a white female use. But I,

Alisha, was indeed segregated throughout my childhood in a hurtful way. It caused horrific childhood trauma. Trauma that took decades to overcome. In no wise am I dismissing the segregation that ethnic groups experience. On the contrary, I am very compassionate toward others because of my unfortunate past. The pain taught me empathy.

School officials had painted the walls of my middle school in different colors for students to stand in various areas to identify them during the transition from class to class. You see, I was required to stand on the school's wall – the brightly painted wall to identify myself as a special education student. Can you imagine the stage of your life that you are going through so much change in middle school? That you are segregated from others? It was so traumatic that I can't even tell you the actual color of the wall for the students with learning challenges like me. All I do know is the blue or green walls were designated for the regular or gifted kids. The bathroom became my chosen place of hiding. That is where I became the resourceful person I am today. In fact, I was so innovative that my classmates did not even know about my challenges with reading comprehension and mathematical computation. Was I not worthy of being treated humanely because my brain processed things differently? There was no one there to champion my cause for me not to be ostracized and belittled. I became my advocate. I learned to hide, and I became the popular kid because I walked my other friends to class so they would never see me go from the dreaded painted wall to the learning disabilities classroom. I became an expert chameleon. But that turned into inner turmoil – I was inauthentic. I felt broken and invisible.

Denial became my best friend and constant companion during middle school and into high school.

Sadly, I wish I could say elementary was any better. It wasn't that was my initiation into escape. Sitting in class was not an option. I roamed the hallways like a determined ant at a picnic; I constantly escaped the structured safety zone for the 'smart kids.' I found peace and freedom outside. There was solace; I was in a safe space. Inside the classroom, I felt strangled and confined. Nothing was secure, even in my favorite teacher's classroom. Joyce Packman, my special education teacher, was devoted to my education, but she was a solo investor. She was excellent, but that was not enough – the hope and joy of regular education escaped me.

Those moments were disruptive to my psyche. I continued to hear in my inner voice that I was not good enough and I was stupid. Then one day, hope arrived. My mentor Debbie Ford came into my life, and I began working for her. As great as she was, she, too, got frustrated with me at times until she understood how my brain worked.

An amazing epiphany overcame me. I was good enough. I was smart in my unique way. I was a visual learner who thrived with kinesthetic experiences that allowed me to chunk my learning and categorize things.

Today I am a successful massage therapist, entrepreneur, and life coach. I dominate in my career choices because they are conducive to my wiring and my learning styles. In addition to working with women, opportunities to work with young people were afforded to me. Using Shadow Work with Debbie Ford, I was able to see my wounds and where they stemmed from; I did not have to be in denial or hide any longer. I found my gifts in the shadow of my pain and trauma. The realization that hope was given to me to be the amazingly compassionate woman that I am. I wouldn't be able to give back to others as I do. That work was redemptive and life changing.

Because I didn't know the disconnect between my head and my heart, I showed up maimed emotionally. However, that made me be the champion for children. Enlightening parents about how to take responsibility for the emotional wellness of their children became my cause. So, if you are a parent, here is a note for you:

Would you please move out of your child's possibilities so they can be the best version of them? Own your part in any limiting beliefs you have cultivated and help them take off the mask and allow the growth.

Maybe you're that parent who has taken that ownership, and you tried to do the best you could, but that was not enough. Let it start today with the conscious decision to be better and be more aware. This will allow you to take more responsibility to help yourself with your gifts that are hovering in the shadow. You can become more authentic and use the shadow instead of allowing the shadow to use you.

I can relate to the children I worked with because my parents had Shadow Work to do. I observed a lot of verbal abuse. My relationship with my father was not strong until Shadow Work unleveled me to my greatness. My wounds were caused by my schooling and my father's behavior, but ultimately, I had to own the repair work. Allowing the good and giftedness to come out of the shadows of hurt, pain, and trauma moved me into growth and development. It was the doorway for forgiveness and a new life of freedom and emotional wholeness.

Today, my dad and I have a great relationship. We are very close; it took some work to get over the abusive ways, but we did it. I had to understand that he was the best he could be. He was abused and never sought help. That wasn't good for me because it made me become a self-abuser and the negative voices were loud and overpowering.

Nevertheless, now those same voices are non-existent. They have no energy. I know unworthiness, thoughts of stupidity, and hopelessness are not my reality. I have hope and power. I am so intelligent and fully visible.

Put the Work In

After our personal inhibitions were overcome, Mother-Daughter Dynamic Duo could be formed. We both became coaches under the tutelage of Debbie Ford and Ford Institute. We made peace with our past and the parts of us that we didn't see as valuable—our gifts. Shadow Work gave us a unique voice to liberate ourselves and offer others life-changing experiences.

These two diamonds in the rough became impactful for our clients. We embraced and owned our forgiveness, love, compassion, power, complete visibility in the world, self-acceptance, and identity. The dreaded imposture syndrome and hopelessness were turned into empowerment. It was a huge blessing for us to not walk in shame and offer women the joy of being a part of a process of forgiving.

Forgiveness is a great foundation. We constantly talk about it. It oozes out of us like a river of water. The Good Book tells us to love and forgive. There is a reason for that - unforgiveness hurts you, not the other person.

Mother-Daughter Dynamic Duo has successfully taught women to have great motherly relationships and connect better with any type of woman-to-woman relationship, whether in business partnerships, on the job, in the family, or with friends.

Simply put, we are just two ordinary ladies who discovered ourselves on an extraordinary journey of self-improvement. We have tried to open the doors for others and make a pathway to walk on with ease. In sharing our story, it is anticipated that this chapter has been enlightening and will open that trail for you to expand your hope and success even more. There is a strength in your self-discovery. Thank you for confronting those overcasting shadows that have or are currently stopping your greatness. Every day is a new opportunity to use God's gift of the present to be better and more excellent. Allow your gifts to have a voice and shine.

ROCHELLE & ALISHA SCHWARTZ

Rochelle and Alisha, mother and daughter themselves, have been Certified Relationship Coaches for 20 years each, for a total of 40 years of experience! They are passionate about working through and healing the issues that mothers and daughters face - and manifesting real "Loving and Thriving" connections between the women in the family! They are the "Mother-Daughter Dynamic Duo.

Website: www.rochelleschwartz.com
Email: coachrochelle@comcast.net or shadowbstr3@yahoo.com
FB: www.facebook.com/relationshipcoachrochelleschwartz
www.facebook.com/AlishaKaraSchwartz

FLOURISH IN YOUR FIRE

" Know you are a light and blessing to others by the gifts instilled in you as you touch their lives" -C. Morgan

Welcome to the hope ignited path and the journey we are on. I want to discuss self-awareness and productivity. Where are you at with your self-awareness and productivity throughout the day? Where do you see any holes? Where do you know where you would like to improve? One thing I look at is we have this fire inside of us. And the fire, at times, can dim down and sometimes can actually go completely out. But we have this smoke, which as long as it keeps smoking, we are good as we continue our productivity. When there is smoke, it's a sign that embers are still burning. As long as you have an ember burning within you, you are ready to ignite. One thing I want to speak on is flourishing the fire you have within.

In 2007, I became homeless unexpectedly after returning from maternity leave to my position as a Financial Counselor and Patient Account Representative. Many assume homelessness looks like an unclean person living on the street. In all actuality, many people live paycheck to paycheck with the possibility of being one paycheck away from being homeless. That is the physical view. Many forget homelessness is also the mental and emotional anguish of an empty shell one can feel. Upon my return to work, I was advised that my position was posted due to a change in management and downsizing without any notification this was occurring in the company. I sat in my office in disbelief. I lost my job due to being downsized. What was I to do? I had two girls, Jaz'min and Sayonie. My youngest daughter was just born. She was only three months old. I just moved into a new place and found myself moving out of this apartment within 30 days.

It was devastating. The fire inside of me went down because I was thinking, "what am I going to do?" I felt like I was on the right path, trying to do the right things for my girls, my family, and for myself to provide a lasting future for them, something for them to savor. This priceless moment in time for me was embarrassing because I didn't want to be homeless. I did not want my children to endure this kind of childhood memory. I began looking for another job; I had to arise from the smoke.

For a brief moment, I stayed with a family member. That didn't work because it was crowded, and my girls were allergic to pets. It just was not viable at the time. I was used to living on my own and being excessively independent. I applied for government assistance and was told I would have to be three months behind before becoming eligible for any kind of assistance. I'm the type of person who always pays my bills ahead to allow myself a cushion in case of an emergency. I could not be proactive and get ahead before turmoil ensued. I had to show I needed help. It wasn't enough to show proof from my employer that the department downsized and a letter from the landlord stating I was no longer living there. The landlord included in the letter a statement indicating since I entered a lease, I was being charged for each month the apartment was not occupied. Again, this was not enough from the apartment management. A letter of eviction was needed. I was infuriated. Everyone knows if you get evicted, it is a blemish and hell trying to obtain another home of residence. I felt I was being punished for having my bills paid in advance, having a job, going to school to enhance my education for a better paying career, and being independent of any help from government services. Now that I needed it, it was a slap in the face of what I had to do to get it. I was down on my luck. No, I don't believe in luck. For me, where my faith is with GOD, GOD had me idle for a while and sit still to see the actual plan I was supposed to be in versus the one I was fighting. My fire was going toward the wrong plan and wrong direction.

By this time, I got a call three days before Christmas from transitional housing; I had applied for months earlier. The accommodation had rules and guidelines to follow. The housing had a limited time before you had to leave the premises. What seemed like a breather was actually a countdown to an expiration date to get things in order in less than a year. A year may seem like a long time. However, it is not at all. I lost everything except my car. Barely holding on to that, but I had to have a place for my children to stay. I needed and wanted so badly to establish some type of stability in the chaotic whirlwind we were in together.

One benefit for the families during this holiday time is the receipt of gifts for the families. There are charitable organizations that donate to the needs of the families. Many organizations partnered with transitional housing to offer essential education in physical, mental, emotional health and wellness, services to unite the family again, counseling, budgeting, and other life skills to get back on their feet to be productive in the community again. I was happy to have a place for the girls to lay their heads, and we were together. My family was not counted in the tally of families. We were a last-minute addition. The ladies Dawn, Dana, and Laura were my angels and blessings. These ladies were able to provide some gifts to give to my children for Christmas. It was nice to know there were still some kind-hearted people in the world, and I did not have to jump through hoops or fight with them to get their kindness. I have always donated and helped families in time of need, no matter what time of year it was. I was blessed to have it returned. I was only in the beginning stages of the battle. I needed to win the war, not for me but for my girls. I needed to show them how to survive in adversity and when life did not seem fair. I was determined not to be subjugated by my circumstances. I was empowered to trailblaze in my fire.

What does it mean to flourish in your own fire? What is the fire to you? What will it do to you? What does a flourishing, vibrant fire look like to you? Is it when you're in a good mood or when things are going well? Take a look at it a different way. Is it pushing you to a new or different level you need to be at? One thing with fire, as you know, it burns, it needs the heat, oxygen, and fuel to keep going. It really needs oxygen to survive. This is similar to our bodies. We need oxygen to survive, or we die physically. We also die internally when we're not feeding and flourishing the fire within us to keep us going. When you find out what that means to you, what keeps you going to keep that fire lit inside to be that productive woman? What are you self-aware of? What are some of the things in your life that you don't want to talk about? What are some fears that you don't want to face? Are those fears and doubts keeping you from being productive? Are they holding you back? Look at it this way, some of the things holding you back at times are the things that will actually release you from where you are at if you're in a stagnant or unproductive situation at the time.

When you're moving forward, the fuel that you need to burn is the oxygen inside of your body, and we need the oxygen to live, and that's the fire. It's simultaneous inside and out. Our spirit needs to flourish too. Our mind, our body, our health all the way around. The overall health we need to flourish and everything that we do. We flourish in our children even if we do not know it. We flourish into strangers by even just saying, "Hi, how are you doing?" Something so simple that puts a smile on somebody's face.

On Earth, gravity determines how that flame burns as we are in the world today. Sometimes we should not always look at how the world ignites and continues our flame flourishing. We should look within ourselves because that's the only thing that matters in the end. Yes, we need each other and can't do things alone by ourselves. We need each other to make a plan, uplift, and work together to give back to the community to flourish and develop in whatever we do. We do need to do that.

At times, the heat itself for the flame keeps the flame at the ignition temperature. What ignition temperature do you have? What gets it going for you? Do you have to be backed into a corner before you break out and move? Do you have to be in a good place to see? The things in your perception and your awareness of yourself have to be you looking positively to move forward? In every situation, there is a negative, and there is a positive. What do you see when you look deep inside your eyes while looking in the mirror? I understand it's not always visible to the naked eye and what we see but are we looking at it in a pessimistic or optimistic view. Take, for instance, when I was discussing when I was homeless. I could have kept that negative mindset. Yes! I had a moment when my reflections in the mirror behind my naked sight told me I was not happy. It made me think I failed my children as a single mother, I was humiliated and embarrassed, and I was disappointed with myself. I live by high expectations and standards. I keep them there as resilience in the face of adversity.

I had to find a silver lining. There were times depression would show its ugly face. I did not have time to cope with my emotions or wallow in self-pity. I could only "do" because no one else was going to provide what I needed. I'm not going to lie to you; many times, at night, I sat and cried, pondering what am I going to do? It was as if, at every turn, there was another obstacle, another demon to conquer. I encourage crying. We all need to pour out the toxicity at times. As my tears rolled down my cheeks and dripped on my chest, they reminded me of raindrops. My tears were cleansing raindrops of water. Water promotes growth, nourishment, and new evolution. If you have to cry to release what's inside of you, cry. When you have so many emotions bottled up inside, you can turn into a toxic volcano waiting to explode. That's not good either, exploding, taking it out on everybody in your path. Allow the smooth river of the emotional release of hurt, anger, frustration, tired of being tired to flow down your face in healing. Have the hard cry to embrace some comfort. As the volcano dies down and you become sleepy, this is equivalent to the fire when it starts to be smoky and smothering out.

What comes of fire is ashes like the Phoenix. You don't want to let it smother out completely, but you always want to rebuild even if it does welter. You are reborn and starting a new path or level. Any prior judgment you were bonded in is no longer clouded. It is eliminated with the clarity of new life and the light filled inside you. You can't change yesterday, but today you live in the now—the present which is the gift given to you daily. Navigate to start again to keep igniting that fire within you.

You may ask, how do I keep my fire ignited? How do I keep the flame moving? How do I keep going day to day, increasing productivity? Check your ignition temperature. Look and discover what motivates you and keeps you procuring momentum. The heat of the flame itself keeps the fuel at the ignition temperature. As long as the fuel is being burned and the oxygen is all around you, and you believe with every breath you breathe, continue to ignite to survive. Surrounding fuel support can be emotional, informational, tangible, self-esteem, belonging, affirmational, self-care, family, associates, colleagues, friends, and your faith base. Even if you do not think you have support in your immediate family, a stranger can support you too. God uses angels and vessels to connect with you to hear Him or whatever your faith may be at the time to keep you going. Because it helps release you, and when that flame ignites, the gases help the fire spread.

Key Elements and Four Stages of a Flourishing Fire

As you are being ignited, fire has key elements and four stages. The critical aspects of fire are:

1. Smoke- Inner Light and Ignition
2. Oxygen- What did GOD breathe into you
3. Fuel- Passion, family, the why that makes you thrive to live
4. Heat- What are strategies in place, energy, self-awareness, productivity

These four elements equal a flourishing fire propagation chain reaction. The four stages of fire include incipient, growth, fully developed, and decay.

The incipient is the dawning, beginning to happen, and developing stage. Ignition has occurred. This is the most crucial point because it has not spread as of yet. This stage can be suppressed instantaneously by the negative feedback received from family and friends when you tell them your plans, goals, or ideas. Because if you listen to it and BELIEVE it, you will kill your fire right after ignition.

The growth stage of the fire is self-sustaining and can be harder to control. You determine what will push you to complete tasks and find your most productive time of day. Many barriers are encountered; self-doubt may succumb to you because you are not allowing yourself hope to stay ignited. Better yet why are you fearful of being successful? Stop getting comfortable in "why does everything come up when things are going well?" Are obstacles arising, or are you allowing your perception to change to see the world you are comfortable in? Be aware of your behavior.

The fully developed stage is when all the fuel is burning. It is at the max and the hottest points are reached. This is the most dangerous because you can find yourself trapped within the fire. All combustible material is being utilized. These are your resources and ideas to resolve any progress to keep moving forward. Here you find your non-negotiables to push past, preventing getting caught in your own thoughts and head.

The actions in the decay stage are rotting and decomposing. The fire runs out of oxygen and fuel to sustain itself. However, do not resist the decaying of a new level of growth. Let that old molding sloth off and embrace the new skin of life and vibrant flourishing fire inside. We have to change our mixture to begin burning bright again and spreading your fire.

And it's ok to start all over again. Don't look at it as you are starting over again with nothing. You are starting over again in a new

Journey, a new level, a new development within yourself being productive. Begin with small goals throughout the day and commit to them. It doesn't have to be something gigantic. I get it; I know some of you like to see quick results, or results, period. Understanding that a small step is better than a giant leap at times when all you can take right then is a small step. The small steps may APPEAR to be insignificant. It is still a progression. It's still flourishing your fire. You're still adding to it. You need wood for the fire. You need oxygen to help burn a fire and to keep it going. What oxygen are you putting back in yourself? What self-development are you giving yourself? What self-growth?

What self-care are you giving yourself to keep that flourishing fire in you to keep it going? I need you to realize that every one of us has a fire that is individually and uniquely personalized in your favor. No one can take that away from you. We take it from ourselves! We smother our own fire when we are trying to be that super parent, great spouse, a partner in a relationship, or phenomenal employee. We take on an immense amount of responsibility. Do not relinquish your power at the hands of the insignificant mindset of an individual who is not contributing to your positive, successful well-being. It is said at times, and we are not given anything we are not ready to handle. We are given many things on our plate to manage, but who said we have to execute each item alone? Evoke your chain reaction to set yourself free and permit yourself to travel through the stages of your sacred fire.

Let's be productive and work smarter to alleviate the

destruction of our body, mind, and soul. We are given much opposition to handle, but we also are given the ability to delegate. We have vessels and resources around us to enact and annihilate the overflow on our plates. Seek help and support.

Realize that each of us has a fire inside and that fire is a gift that is an imperfectly perfect masterpiece. No one can take that away from you. Our gift will make room for us. When God is satisfied with the seeds we are planting, He will bring the vessels to us to help us cultivate our life. We are not given tomorrow, only a present moment to flourish in our fire. Be aware of who you are, what your fire is, and the impact you can have on others. The path has been ignited, and our journey is illuminated with a flourished fire uniquely provided to us. Believe YOU are the gift to set yourself free and on fire!

Flourishing Fire Mantra:

God doesn't give me what I can handle; God helps me handle what I am given. I am one of many that He covers and anoints immensely to embrace what the world throws at my strength and beacon of light. I am the enemy's opposition. Keep making him bow at God's powers and miracles performed through me. I am God's creation! No one or thing will ever conquer or bewilder me with the faith-filled heart, spirit, and soul that thrives inside me."

C MORGAN

C Morgan uses her knowledge as a certified DISC consultant and behavior analyst in her Life Coaching business. Her work changes the lives of those around her, and her area of specialty is personal and professional development coaching. She is a mother of two, mental health and wellness advocate, and a licensed nurse.

HOPE THROUGH HEALING: ON A COMMUNITY AND INDIVIDUAL LEVEL

We are in some tumultuous times, not only with this deadly outbreak but even more so within our broken communities. We see mothers and fathers lose their children to violence, being snatched away from the family nucleus-SUDDENLY. We see the continuation of poverty plaguing our communities, and wherever we see poverty, we can find its correlating buddy, CRIME. And let's not forget the evil pandemic of racism that still reeks from the soul and foundation of America. This hatred that we continue to see has many effects on us all, and many ask, "Do we have anything to hope for?" "Will this world ever be this better place that everyone keeps talking about?" Those are great questions. Let's dive a little deeper.

What if I told you that the answer to all your questions lives deep within? What if you've been searching for answers, only to find that they've been with you all along. When we talk about healing a community, we must first start with the individual. When we look at the problems that plague our communities, it's easier to paint the picture not to include us as a part of the problem. Well, guess what; when we do this, we miss the opportunity to find the proper solution because the solution wouldn't include us either. And I get it, sometimes looking inside of ourselves is hard. It's hard to see how we contribute to our own stagnancy, thus keeping us from adequately showing up for the community.

Now I know that somebody is wondering what that looks like. I was once in that seat of blindness. It's a place of comfort. It's a place where defense mechanisms have helped you resiliently rest in your area of stagnancy. See, I created a shell of a person and kept showing up, but it showed out most times. It's easy to act out of character when you don't see the royalty that radiates in your soul. Life experiences have blinded many of our lights. Life experiences have killed many of our dreams. And yet we keep climbing, just not sure of our destination. And although this place of comfort (your broken place hidden away) is one of false peace, the need for healing and manifesting greatness is bursting from the inside, ready to be released.

So, we're back to "what does this look like?" Everyone needs a blueprint. The blueprint remains the same, but each of our experiences manifests differently throughout the process. Okay, brace yourself. This first step is hard. It's one that you'll have to repeat over and over and over again.

Step 1: _LOOK IN THE MIRROR: SELF-AWARENESS IS THE NEW SELF-CARE_

Now say it with me! No wait, as a matter of fact, go look in the mirror right now and proclaim this new declaration over your life, "SELF-AWARE IS THE NEW SELF-CARE." This simply means that becoming one with you is imperative. Knowing who you are, good, bad, sometimes ugly, is imperative to this process. It's accepting your '_now_' but leaving your heart open for the newness of what's ahead. When you are in the space of self-awareness, you find yourself learning and growing better every day. When you are self-aware, you understand it's about gaining the lessons needed so that you won't repeat the same mistakes over and over again. This new place is where healing takes place, from the inside out. This is where YOUR LIGHT begins to shine bright. And, if you stay in that place of continual growth, you will be well on your way to your purpose/alignment/oneness with the GOD in you. You will be in tune with the HOPE THAT LIES WITHIN.

Okay, so now we're looking inside of ourselves, what do we do next? Well, I'm glad you asked! There's another step to complete. Please be clear about something here, there are many steps. There are multiple places that we must go while we're on this road to your destiny. Someone can share their blueprint, but it's up to you to see your way through. You will begin to discover your steps, the same steps that GOD ordered for you. You are the captain of your ship, and with the HOLY SPIRIT leading the way, you are sure never to go wrong.

> *Sidebar: I didn't say you won't do wrong because **NONE** of us are perfect. We will have a lifetime of growing better.*

Okay, I digress. One of the next steps for me was very instrumental and still is to this very day. You need this component like you need the air you breathe. Are you ready? Ready or not…

STEP 2: YOU MUST DEAL SO THAT YOU CAN CONTINUE TO HEAL

Dealing with life's experiences can be extremely difficult, especially when life/people have violated you. But in this place, the blueprint calls for us to deal with these pains, traumas, or whatever deep hurts are locked away into the core of our beings. This part won't be easy. This part will send you through a whirlwind of emotions. This part will be more painful than you realize. But this pain is different. It's not like that stagnancy of pain that's been floating deep within. This pain mimics the recovery process after a successful surgery. The pain is there, but it gets better every day. You get stronger every day. Your resilience is moving in a helpful direction. You're well on your way, down the road to recovery, whatever that looks like for you. Forward-thinking, forward movement, upward bound! When we lose the baggage of what we hide within, we free ourselves to walk in the truth of who we are and answer the question of our purpose. Let's move on to step number three.

STEP 3: _IT'S WHATEVER YOU NEED IT TO BE, YOUR DESTINY IS UP TO YOU_

Whatever you want to do, with your life, you can do it. Whatever dreams you see, you can manifest them. Whatever steps you're designed to take, you will walk that path and do it with excellence. All it takes is for you to believe that it's true. It all starts in your mind. When your mind, heart, body, and soul reach the place of alignment, you will manifest whatever greatness that lies deep within. In this place, the more you dig deep inside that continual pruning process, the more you'll find the keys to the treasures needed to complete your life's assignment. Dig deep. JOY is waiting there. HOPE is waiting there. There you will find PEACE!

So, we've talked about individual healing, but what does that mean for the community? Great question. Let's explore it together. Community simply means folks who live around each other, who may also have kindred interests, meaning they have a common bond. However, when we think about community, we must examine community members. Community members make up the sum of the community. They are the nucleus of the area, the heart, the soul, the backbone of whatever the community reflects and represents. There are so many things that happen within our communities that reflect the tragedy of a broken soul. From that individual perspective, if one shows up in the community, in that broken place, certain behaviors could cause one to hurt folks just because they are hurting. Someone who shows up in that broken place cannot be a light for the children who are watching and observing.

The solution is an easy fix, but the work isn't easy. If the individual is healed, the community is healed - one person at a time. This empowerment comes from within. No one can give it to us. As empowerment spreads, we take control of any force that seeks to destroy the community bond we are working to build. The stronger everyone becomes, individually, the stronger and more effective our unit will be when we unite and show up in that space with one another - on one accord. The more we fall into alignment with ourselves, the more we can extend grace to those who haven't reached the place their soul desires or longs to be. The only way to have a solid community is for us ALL to stand together. Whatever we do, whether it's fighting against racism or finding the kind of empowerment we need to thrive as a community. WE MUST DO IT TOGETHER!!

Community bonding is an "ALL HANDS-ON DECK" approach. We must lay down our biases we hold and respect each other. We must respect each other's differences because each difference was crafted and created to fit into the beautiful puzzle of community. We each play our role and play a huge part in cultivating and sustaining a thriving community. We are all accountable for the changes we need to see. We are responsible for the road ahead. Our children depend on the outcomes of togetherness and the world we can create by standing together as one. We can do it. We must take ownership of the role we play and play it well. It may start with you, but it ends with COMMUNITY!!

TRISCHE' DUCKWORTH

Trische' cries loud and spares not. She is a social worker by trade, but typical walls don't confine her; she is a ministry without walls type of servant. Trische resides in Michigan and is the executive director and founder of the 501(c)(3) nonprofit Survivors Speak and director of programming and outreach for SOOAR.

To learn more about Survivor's Speak and how you can participate in the transformative change of communities or donate to the cause, go to: https://www.survivorsspeak.info/about

You cannot hope to build a better world without improving the individuals. To that end, each of us must work for his own improvement and, at the same time, share a general responsibility for all humanity, our particular duty being to aid those to whom we think we can be most useful. - **Marie Curie**

MY JOURNEY OF HOPE
TO MINDFULNESS PROSPERITY

My journey of hope is action; my hope is not just a thought to wish for in life. But, before we begin, what does hope mean? In the dictionary, hope is a feeling of expectation, a desire for something to happen with anticipation, to want something to happen or be true. My journey of hope is to be true, and manifest what I need, deserve, and want. Prosperity, in the dictionary, is the condition of being successful or thriving, usually by making a lot of money. Most people associate prosperity with finances or wealth.

On the other hand, I see prosperity as good health, happiness from within, and peacefulness. My road to prosperity is growing spiritually, mentally, and emotionally. My mindfulness prosperity is connecting to the one God through self-development and challenging my fears.

To do this, I need to start with my childhood, where the foundation begins but does not end. I am the youngest of three children and the only girl. I was extremely shy, very timid, but most of all, I stuttered severely to the point that I did not talk and could not talk. I just hoped that the pain of being bullied and teased would just stop, but it did not. I had to create a space of peacefulness, and that was through praying and sleeping. When I got a good night's rest, I noticed that I felt so much better about myself. Sleep was an escape for me like a vacation is to someone who needs to unwind, relax, or just get away. In the process of doing this, I was hoping to have enough strength to deal with the situation every day.

While in high school, I did not participate in anything for fear of stuttering. I felt so inadequate, and I hoped my classmates did not know I stuttered severely. If I opened my mouth, the children would laugh. I just sat there, quiet and lonely. I had no confidence, and my self-esteem was extremely low. The internal pain felt like I had no place in life, no voice, just inner silence. This situation dominated my life until my mid-thirties and beyond.

Of course, my teenage years were not any better. I had to deal with severe acne from the age of sixteen to twenty-five. I was called every name you could think of bumpy face, pie face, and so on. I already felt low because of my severe stuttering and shyness. This internal crisis was so overwhelming. I felt depressed most of the time. But thank God, my depression was a blessing because it was during this time I reflected on God. I now realize God's had a purpose for me in that stage of my life.

Fast forward, working at many jobs over the years was a challenge in itself but a blessing of faith and trust. Yes, I was a job hopper in my mid-twenties. Hey, don't judge me because all those trials made me the person I am today, not afraid to take chances in life and make changes. If I can do it with my stuttering and shyness, you can create your own journey of hope to mindfulness prosperity. Oh, back to my job challenges. If I did not feel like I would be promoted based on my experience, no job growth, or didn't like how I was being treated, I would quit. Of course, that does not mean I am a quitter, but I value my health and peace of mind. My philosophy was my health was more important than a job. I did not just hope for a better job; I took action all the time and just left and found another job time after time.

First, I never understood how I would get jobs at the drop of a hat, so to speak. Second, I mastered job interviews like I was an award-winning academy actress. Third, I always knew when things were not going to work out at my previous jobs. I sometimes felt like I was the employee in a group home that no one wanted or cared about. I did not fit in any click. I was always told you are not a fit even though it was never my job performance that was an issue. I always felt like an outcast. But I was not fearful of losing my job because I answered to God. Remember, I had plenty of experience quitting but not a quitter.

On the other hand, once I quit, I felt so happy and relieved; I was free from employee abuse. In reality, I was winning. Therefore, I always decided to quit before they would have the pleasure of firing me. That's faith, especially when I was a single parent with my place and plenty of bills to pay. It takes guts to quit a job and step out on faith time after time. As a result of quitting my job when I felt depressed or stressed, I had severe anxiety. I did not feel appreciated, and it took its toll on me financially. I had to file bankruptcy three or four times, and I stopped counting. It was not because I did not pay my bills when I had a job but because of the inconsistency of money flowing in to pay them monthly. The bottom line was I did not care about the jobs. I have always believed in God and myself, and I just did it. I did not realize I had the entrepreneurial spirit in me by taking risks when most people were afraid to leave their job. I had heard of people having heart attacks, strokes, and being so unhappy. I said that was not going to be me.

As time moved on, I had a son. He was premature and weighed 1 lb. and 12 ½ ounces. He was severely sick with bleeding in the brain; his lungs collapsed, oxygen for his lungs could have blinded him, and so much more. He was in the hospital for 109 days. He was diagnosed as developmentally delayed and mildly retarded. I had to find the strength to raise my son alone with no help. I became his advocate and fought for his rights and against the injustice, he experienced in school.

Even though I did not speak because I stuttered, I had to find a way to protect and educate myself about my son. That is when I realized I had a voice because I had to educate the educators even though my son was in a special education school until he was 13 years old. I was told that he would not be capable of earning a high school diploma. However, I treated my son like a normal child as much as I could. Today, I am proud to say that my son graduated from regular high school at 18 years old like everyone else. Eight years later, I had a healthy baby girl that was almost premature but, thank God that did not happen. My purpose in sharing this is to instill in you that your circumstances are not your future but your destiny and road map to greatness. Your determination, passion, and purpose are what will lead you through all your trials throughout the various seasons of your life.

When I was 21years old, I was hit by the entrepreneurial bug, but not a real one. Over the years, I tried many network marketing businesses that did not work for me, but I learned from each experience. I realized I was an introvert, and I had a difficult time approaching people. I had more failures than successes, but I did not allow that to stop me from becoming the entrepreneur I was born to be. In my 40 years as an entrepreneur, I must admit that I was successful at two businesses: selling Avon and being a bookkeeper. That was a total of approximately five years. Even though I did not make money from all the other businesses, I consider myself a success because I never gave up; I always had hope. Success is not always making money but for improving yourself through self-development to be the best authentic you.

Today, I am living my best life. I love myself unconditionally, and I like who I am becoming. My confidence, self-worth, and not allowing others to control or dedicate my future has freed me from the past emotional and mental bondage I suffered from for years. I am living my passion and purpose by educating TIRED entrepreneurs, leaders, and professionals about becoming mindful, gaining energy, and being more productive to grow their businesses.

I am a Certified Sleep Science Coach and Certified Holistic Life Coach specializing in sleep, health, and wellness. I love to connect and build relationships. Most of all, I love to educate, enlighten and encourage on why to RESPECT sleep while making sleep a priority. When you are ready to take that step, reach out to me at www.peaceandprosperityinc.com or www.Donata10K.com. This is where you can find all my podcast episodes, "Rest Leads to Revenue," and all my social media information under this one platform.

I am successful as a result of all the self-development courses, books, programs, coaches, networking events, and so much more. I am happy to share; I am now a three-time author, National Editor of The National Black Unity News, a Podcast host, and believe it or not, a paid speaker.

Today is the day you discover and walk into your journey of hope to your own mindfulness and prosperity.

WAKE UP WITH HOPE

Happy with who God created you to be. He makes no mistakes!!!

Optimistic about your future and the plans God has for your life.

Putting on the whole armor of God, so you can handle anything that comes your way.

Embracing God and His promises, faith is the substance of things hoped for and the evidence of things not seen.

What is hope?

Hope is an optimistic state of mind based on an expectation of positive outcomes with respect to events and circumstances in one's life or the world at large. As a verb, its definitions include: "expect with confidence" and "to cherish a desire with anticipation." Wikipedia

What does hope mean in the Bible?

"Hope" is commonly used to mean "a wish": its strength is the strength of the person's desire. But in the Bible, hope is the confident expectation of what God has promised, and its strength is in His faithfulness.

Why is hope important?

Hope gives us something to strive for. When we envision a better life for ourselves, hope gives us the strength to do what we must do to make it happen. Hope reduces feelings of helplessness, increases happiness, reduces stress, and improves our quality of life.

I want to share a story of hope that helped me heal from a painful relationship and look forward to a blessed and beautiful future. In July 1999, on a bright sunny Sunday, the kids and I were excited about preparing a birthday dinner for their dad, my then-fiancée. (Let's call him Markel to protect the not-so-innocent). At that time, Rockie and Mackey were three years old, and Jeremy was twelve. To put it in context, I did not have twin girls, but Markel had fathered a child in an outside relationship, and my daughter (Rockie) and Mackey were four months apart in age. I agreed to have Mackey live with us after her mother's tragic death and treated her as if she were my own. Jeremy is my son from a previous relationship.

This particular Sunday, Markel went to church services in his hometown, and the kids and I went to our usual church service. After church, the kids and I took a trip to the store to buy a new grill and all the fixings for our dinner surprise. We all loved grill day. Grill day included music, dancing, playing games; the girls helped me prep in the kitchen, and Jeremy helped on the grill.

When we returned home from shopping, the girls helped me prep the side dishes, and Jeremy helped prep the meat. Awaiting

Markel's arrival, I put the girls down for a nap, and Jeremy joined his friends for their usual bike riding adventures. In the meantime, I was on the phone having a conversation with my godson's father. He shared the incidences that resulted in him getting temporary custody of his boys and the custody battle he was preparing for. During the call, Markel returned home. Overhearing the conversation, Markel apparently assumed that a part of that conversation was in reference to him and Jeremy when it was about my godson and his mother's (then) guy friend. I later learned that Markel had displayed some similar behaviors with Jeremy unknown to me.

After I completed the call and was still excited about the surprise dinner, we had planned. Suddenly, I was confronted with yelling, accusations, and blows to my head and body. Obviously drunk, Markel continued to punch me in various areas of my face and body. Nothing I said or did could get him to stop. It was as if he was possessed. My 5'5" medium stature became bloody and limp at the hands of a 6'4" angry man. In response to Rockie begging him to stop, he became distracted long enough for me to pull his tie in a way that would cause it to tighten around his neck. Holding on to the tie with the weight of my body became too much for him to bear, and he finally stopped punching me. While he took my daughter out of the room, I was able to get to the phone and call the police. I assume he returned to the room to finish the job, but he immediately left the house when he realized I was on the phone with the police.

When EMS and the police arrived, they promptly began attending to my wounds and settling the girls. By then, Mackey had awakened, not knowing what had happened. Shortly after the police arrived, Jeremy returned home to find me bloody and bruised. He already knew who harmed me; he ran out of the house, jumped on his bike in search of Markel. Imagine the humiliation and pain of having to sit through the questioning, picture taking, and not being able to leave the "scene" to go after my son. I charged the police officers to go after him, or they would have to arrest me to keep me there.

After all the drama had ceased and the parade of strangers was gone, I was still left to care for Mackey since Markel left her there. I soon contacted her maternal grandmother and informed her of what had happened.

Fast forward, about a month and a half later, I woke up to tender breast and extreme nausea. Fearing that I was pregnant, I ran to the store for a home pregnancy test, and the results were positive. I scheduled an appointment to confirm the test results and learned I was, in fact, pregnant. I had fallen into such a deep depression; I had mistaken pregnancy symptoms for symptoms of depression. Devastated with the news, I tearfully told my doctor I could not go through with it. With the abortion planned, the visions and sounds of the ultrasound strolling in my head would not let me go through with it. B is 21 years young today, and I cannot imagine life without him.

While this story has so many more components, I believe I have told enough for you to get the picture. I was in a really low place, feeling hopeless and helpless. I felt that life had dealt me an unfair blow. I shared this story not to depress you but to give you hope. It took H.O.P.E. to bring me through and out of this ugly situation. It's often said, *hope springs eternal*, but I am sure we can all agree that it does not always feel that way. Experiencing the feeling of helplessness can haunt us. It can be devastating when we struggle with intense emotions like anxiety, anger, depression, or even worse, a significant loss or turmoil in a relationship. Here's one that we've all experienced either directly or indirectly: the overwhelming feeling of extreme uncertainty when the COVID-19 pandemic spanned the globe. Many were plagued with hopelessness and helplessness. I am here to tell you that there is hope even when things seem they are at their worst.

My great grandmother (lovingly called Mama by her great-grandchildren and Boss by her grandchildren) used to say, "behind every dark cloud is a silver lining." Although she explained what that meant, my young mind was not mature enough to embrace that concept. When bad things happened, I found it difficult to find anything good about it. I often experienced feelings of anger, disappointment, embarrassment, failure, hurt, and hopelessness. But what I did know, even in my youth, Mama had a very strong relationship with the Lord. As a Bible-believing, God-fearing adult, I now can embrace the concept and can boldly say, "BUT GOD!" God will see us through any test that comes our way. All we must do is believe and trust in Him.

"At least there is hope for a tree: If it is cut down, it will sprout again, and its new shoots will not fail. It's roots may grow old in. the ground and its stump die in the soil, yet at the scent of water it will bud and put forth shoots like a plant." Job 14:7-9

Do you remember the story of Job? Job endured unthinkable

difficulties, afflictions in his mind and body, major losses, including family, friends, and everything he owned. Yet, he held on to hope and his steadfast faith in God. Even in the saddest of moments and the hardest of times, know that God has you covered. Knowing and believing in God's Word will give you comfort and remind you of the power and resilience you have through His Holy Spirit.

I spent many tearful days and nights while going through my storm. There were days when I felt so low and alone; I did not bathe or eat. I often cried out to God and fell limp when I thought He was not hearing or listening to me. I even blamed myself for all the hell I was going through and the pain that seemed never to leave. And for a while, I thought God was disappointed and turned His back toward me. But thank God for a praying mother and all the prayer warriors she, close friends, and family deployed on my behalf. Their prayers most certainly reached God and covered me. I am a witness that there is power in prayer. And when we are too weak and discouraged to pray for ourselves, we can indeed be strengthened by the prayer power of others. It was their prayers that helped me to hear God's voice saying, "this is not the life I planned for you, daughter. I come that you have life more abundantly. I made you in My image, and you are fearfully and wonderfully made." As the days went by, God kept reminding me that He was always with me and that He would be with me through the pregnancy and beyond. I began to have daily conversations with God. Through these conversations and reading God's Word, I was strengthened, and my hope was restored. So, I say to you, no matter what you're going through, God's instruction may not be easy, but it certainly is simple:

"Trust in the Lord with all your heart and lean not to your own understanding; in all your ways submit to Him, and He. Will make your paths straight." Proverbs 3:5-6

I want to encourage you to hold fast to God's unchanging hand and wake up with H.O.P.E. each day and watch God work out His promises in your life. It may not happen immediately but know that it will come to pass.

"But those who Hope in the Lord will renew their strength. They will soar on wings. Like eagles, they will run and not grow weary." Isaiah 40:31

My prayer for you is …

To wake up: **H**appy with who God created you to be. According to Psalm 139:14, David said, "I praise You because I am fearfully and wonderfully made; your works are wonderful, I know that full well." In Psalm 139, David declares that God knows everything we are going to think or say, even before we think or say them. The words that come out of our mouths result from the words that we see in our minds. The words in our minds are a result of our thoughts. Knowing that God already knows what we will think or say before we do it, we should be more careful and deliberate with our thoughts and words. Our words should be inspiring, empowering, and beneficial. Colossians 4:6 says: "Let your conversation be always full of grace, seasoned with salt, so you may know how to answer everyone."

In the world, we are surrounded by so many salty words and thinking. Lies, foul language, and words that are meant to tear us down are all around us. We must resist the temptation to engage in this corrupt behavior. We should hold fast to God's Word and speak words that edify others. This is not just how we should be with our brothers and sisters, but we should also speak words to empower ourselves. In the words of Madea, "It's not what people call you, but it's what you answer to." Remember, you are God's masterpiece, and you must declare every day, "I am fearfully and wonderfully made!"

To wake up: **O**ptimistic about your future and the plans God has for your life.

"For I know the plans I have for you; declares the Lord, plans to prosper you and not to harm you, plans to gave you hope and a future." Jeremiah 29:11

I declare and decree that your best days are ahead of you. Now, I need you to stop right now, put your right hand over your heart and say, "Lord, I thank You that my best days are ahead of me." Let me tell you, the pain; disappointment so blinded me. I had feelings of failure and fear, I could not see beyond that wall of confusion the devil helped me to build. BUT GOD!!! God had different plans for my life. God began to place people in my life and even used some that were already in my life to help chisel away that wall until it was gone. It gave me the power and the hope to get through my pregnancy with a feeling of peace and joy that only God could provide. I was so refreshed, my skin became clearer, my hair was healthy, and my soul rejoiced about the goodness of God. I fell in love with God all over again.

"And we know that for those who love God, all things work together for the good of those who are called according to his purpose." Romans 8:28 (ESV)

I encourage and even implore you to fall in love with and love God unconditionally. He's the source of everything we could ever need or want. God's love for us is unconditional. We are all guilty of displacing our love on people who only love us with conditions, and we spend our time and energy trying to please them. The catch is, we never know when or if they will ever be satisfied. Yet, we keep trying. To satisfy God, all we have to do is view our relationship with Him the same way that He does. From God's perspective, our relationship with Him is based on love, not rules. Think about the parent-child relationship. We give our kids instructions or rules to abide by. When they make mistakes, we still love them and encourage them to grow from their mistakes. We do not stop loving them because they fall short. Well, it's the same with God, our Father. He encourages us to do our best, forgives our transgressions, and instructs us to keep growing. All we have to do is follow His instructions. He tells us precisely what pleases Him, and guess what, y'all, we don't even have to guess whether or not God is pleased with us. God shows us by delivering on His promises if we just obey His word. God is not a man that He should lie. God's request is simple:

"Take delight in the Lord, and He will give you the desires of your heart."
Psalm 37:4

Note to self: Do not cross oceans for those who won't even jump over a puddle for you! Know your worth, and then add tax!!!

To wake up: **P**utting on the whole armor of God, and all His righteousness, so that you can handle ANYTHING that comes your way.

While in my wilderness, I learned that I was dealing with spiritual warfare. Knowing and accepting this reality, I knew I could not fight this battle alone. Even more, I knew that God Himself tells us that the battle is not ours, but His. And God is so amazing that He does not give us what we need to fight the battle because that's His job. Yet, He gives us what we need to stand firm through the battle and conquer whatever the forces of evil bring our way. So, no matter what you are going through, know that God's got you. 2 Chronicles 20:15 says, *"This is what the Lord says to you: Do not be afraid nor discouraged because of this vast army. For the battle is not yours, but God's."*

So, you see, we don't even have to fight the battle ourselves. God's got that covered. But what we must do is trust God and His Word and lean not to our own understanding. Put it all in God's hands and leave it there. In Ephesians 6, God has already given us what we need to stand up to the enemy.

> *"Finally, be strong in the Lord and in His mighty power. Put on the full armor of God, so that you can take your stand against the devil's schemes. For our struggle is not against flesh and blood, but against the rulers, against the authorities, against the powers of the dark world and against the spiritual forces of evil in the heavenly realms. Therefore, put on the full armor of God, so that when the day of evil comes, you may be able to stand your ground and after you have done everything, to stand, stand form then, with the belt of truth buckled around your waist, with the breastplate of righteousness in place, and with your feet fitted with the readiness that comes from the gospel of peace. In addition to all this, take up the shield of faith, with which you can extinguish all the flaming arrows of the evil one. Take the helmet of salvation and the sword of the Spirit, which is the*

Word of God. And pray in the Spirit on all occasions with all kinds of prayers and requests. With this in mind, be alert and always keep on praying for all the Lord's people.
Ephesians 6:10-18

I can hear many of you in my ear right now saying, "Wow, she had to say all that?" Well, yes, I did, and I did so deliberately. I wanted this entire scripture to be in your spirit right now. I did not want to rely on you doing it later. That's just how important it is to me for you to understand and have God's protection. We have to stay girded up daily, and we must understand precisely how to do it. I prayed this scripture of Psalm 91 as well as over my home and family every day so that we would remain under God's protection.

In these scriptures, I found my strength to stand up to Markel when he tried to destroy my reputation and scare me with his threats. The more I made these scriptures a part of my life, the harder it became and more challenging for him to have so much control over me and my emotions. God blessed me with a level of peace that, at one time, seemed impossible to experience. I humbly ask you to trust God and be guided by His instructions. The instructions are the Word of God. Our faith comes from hearing, understanding, and believing the word of God.

"I will instruct you and teach you in the way you should go, I will counsel you with my eye on you." Psalm 32:8

To wake up: **E**mbracing God and His promises. First, we must repent, accept God as our Lord and Savior, and be baptized in His sweet Holy Spirit. If you really are ready for a new life in Christ, I invite you to.

Pray this prayer:

Heavenly and Almighty Father, I come before you with all humility and say I am sorry. I am aware of my sins, and I am ready to repent. Lord, forgive me of my sins and create in me a clean heart and renew a right spirit within me. Lead me to walk in your way, and leave my old life behind, and embrace a new life in You. In the mighty and matchless name of Jesus, I pray! Amen!

Now you are ready to receive God's instructions and promises for your life. Before you can stand on God's promises, you have to know His promises. While God has many promises that have been tested and proven, I want to share a few that have helped me through tough times.

Knowing that God loves us no matter what helped me not feel so helpless and ashamed to ask for His help. I am comforted knowing that God is everything I need in every situation. He is our comforter when we feel alone. He's our healer when we feel pain in our mind, body, or spirit. He's our friend when we are friendless. He's our father when we are fatherless. He's our mother when we are motherless. He's our lawyer in the courtroom. He's our way maker when there seems to be nowhere to turn. God is always with us. It's just that simple—all we have to do is call on God, and He will answer and be there with us.

"For I am convinced that neither death nor life, neither angels nor demons, neither the present Norse the future, nor any powers, neither height, nor depth, nor anything else in all creation, will be able to separate us from the love of God that is in Christ Jesus our Lord." Romans 8:38-39

I implore you to stay in the presence of God so that you can receive the joy of the Lord and His power.

"For the Spirit of God gave us does not make us timid, but gives us power, love and self-discipline." 2 Timothy. 1:7

"You make known to me the path of life; you will fill me with joy in your presence, with eternal pleasures at your right hand.." Psalm 16:11

Being empowered with God's joy and power gives you a sense of peace that is really beyond what we can think or imagine. And the joy of the Lord is your strength to overcome any obstacle that stands in the way of the plans that God has for your life. Believing and standing on God's word opens the door for so many possibilities. You just have to remember that God always has our best interest at heart, and He will never leave us nor forsake us. Believing and standing on God's promises helped me find strength in His presence; I believe in the power I have through Him. I was able to overcome the pain and disappointment. I was experiencing and grew closer in my relationship with God.

"So do not fear, for I am with you, do not be dismayed, for I am your God. I will strengthen you, and help you, I will uphold you with my righteous right hand." Isaiah 41:10

TRUST GOD!!!

I say that with a shout because God is the ONLY one we can depend on, without fail, always to be true to His word. While our family and friends mean well and often do their best to be there for us, they too fall short of their intentions. We often put faith in men and blindly trust that they will follow through on their promises. I am here to tell you, with all humility, trust and have faith in God. Let us hold unswervingly to the hope we profess, for He who promised is faithful like Hebrews 10:23 encourages us to do.

Please pray this prayer with me:

Lord, I love you, and I know that you are my hope. Your word says that you are the hope for the hopeless. I run to you now, with outstretched arms ready and wanting to embrace you. Help me to be happy with who you have created me to be. Lord, give me the discernment and the wisdom to be optimistic and know Your plans for my life. Lord, bestow on me, Your strength and wisdom to withstand the tricks of the enemy. Above all, I pray you to help me to stay in Your will and in Your way. Lord, I want to rest in Your arms and Your love, believing in every promise that I know You are faithful to perform. These and all prayers I pray in the mighty and matchless name of Jesus!!! Amen!!!

NOW, GO BE AMAZING ON PURPOSE!!!

VALERIE FABRE WILLIAMS

Valerie Fabre Williams, or Coach Val as most people call her, is an extreme execution coach and financial coach. She is a certified Christian counselor, certified Game Changers speaker through Eric Thomas, Dave Ramsey Financial Coach, and certified DISC consultant. She is a devoted and loving wife, mother, and grandmother. The eradication of domestic violence, emotional traumas, and sexual abuse impels her. She is the founder of The Purple Rose Consulting Services.
https://www.fabre-williamsenterprisesllc.com

Hope begins in the dark, the stubborn hope that if you just show up and try to do the right thing, the dawn will come. You wait and watch and work: you don't give up. - **Anne Lamott**

KEEP HOPE ALIVE

As I began to think about the title of this book, my mind began to wonder about the word hope and what it really meant. In my mind, all I could come up with a strong desire or want. I looked up the definition it said the meaning of hope with a feeling of expectation and desire for certain things to happen.

Often in our lives, we find ourselves in a situation that has caused us to hope that certain things would go a specific way. As I look back over the many years of my life, I'm so thankful for what all God has done, even when there were times that I thought that all hope was lost. God knows every day I haven't been perfect according to my way of thinking, but as I've come into this place of understanding, God's ways are not our ways, nor His thoughts are thoughts.

Growing up in a Pentecostal in the Church of God in Christ, I thought the rules and practices were absolutely too strict and horrible. At the time, I didn't understand that it wasn't so much about the rules in place, but the discipline set in place and yielding to something greater than ourselves. As I got older, of course, getting out on my own, I began to experience life in an entirely different way. Very much different than how I was raised.

One of the most trying and troubling times of this stage in my early adulthood was my experimentation with drugs. I had never even touched or thought about drugs. That was just an absolute no-no in my world. Who would've ever considered this young, sanctified girl that grew up wearing dresses and skirts every day would do such a thing? The one who couldn't go to the movies or the parties and join in with what all the other kids were doing. She was the girl that was in church for what seemed like every single day. Who would have ever thought that she would even think about touching or getting involved with anything or anyone connected to drugs one day?

Well, that girl was me, and my drug of choice was crack cocaine. Why did I say my drug of choice? I liked what I did. During this time, I smoked marijuana, but I wasn't so crazy about it because I smoked it and then desired to go to sleep. Or, if I smoked too much, I would get sick. So that was not my choice.

Yeah, that was the company I was keeping. I can remember the first time I tried crack cocaine. I thought I would die; my heart was beating so fast, yet I believed in He, which was greater in me not to allow me to die. And every time He did. I felt like I didn't have a problem because I never smoked a "crack pipe." My choice was to smoke what we called "laced cigarettes" and roll it like a joint. I can remember trying it again and again. Repeatedly. You would have thought from the first time I would've had enough. Still, we sometimes do things, and God allows us, or instead, His mercy sees us through. His love guides us through situations that we promise never to do again. But we may turn right around and dig back into it the same thing, figuring it will be different.

I remember saying to myself, I like this, so I began to do it more and more. See, I called myself a functional smoker, meaning I still went to work, took care of my bills, and loved to dress. But how many of us know that you may like something and that something doesn't like you. Come on, somebody, and talk back to me. I know you are reading, but I just need you to say something.

After a while, what I was doing began to affect everything around me, my marriage, attitude, and finances - of course, I was spending large amounts of money. I read something recently that put me back in the mind of the choices that I had made. It said you can't defeat your demons if you're still enjoying their company. In the middle of my addition, I entertained the demons tearing away at me and calling that my one time. Those *one times* continued. However, at the same time, I was crying after God and agonizing in my folly.

I would get high and cry out, saying, "I don't want to do this!" Something more significant in me was saying that this is not who you are. Other times I would be in the company of others smoking and drinking, and I would hear that still small voice saying, you don't belong here. Everything in me began to seem different because I knew that this wasn't my life. Even in what appeared to be the most adverse situation, there was still hope. 2 Corinthians 4:18

says, *so we fix our eyes not on what is seen but on what is unseen since what is seen is temporary but what is unseen is eternal.*

We have an infinite God that never leaves us or forsakes us. He said in Jeremiah 29:11

Let us hold unswervingly to the hope we profess, for he who promised is faithful.

God already had a plan for my life, and He was one for yours. We just must look beyond our present circumstances or obstacles and put our trust and HOPE in Him. I want you to believe that there isn't anything beyond what you may be dealing with or have dealt with that God does not control. I know He is in control, and He will carry you through. It's my testimony.

Crying out God continuously, He answered me because the urges had become undesirable, and He heard me. He saw I was no longer happy in that space and was ready to accept the change. I didn't want to keep saying this is my 'last time' then return to it again the next day. That deliverance day came, and I stood up and said no more. I remember gathering my rolling papers and cigarettes, throwing them in the trash, and taking them out to the dumpster. My mind will never forget that joyous day over 13 years ago.

God saw my heart, and of course, He does know the heart. He knows when it's true and when it's not. He knew that day I was ready to respond to the call that He had so mercifully opened up to me even before I was born. He thought of every part of me. The Bible confirms this in Jeremiah 1:5: *before I formed thee in the womb, I knew thee.* God spoke to the prophet Jeremiah and told him that He had set him apart and appointed him before entering his mother's womb and this world. The same goes for every one of us; God has given us all something to do on earth, even through troubles and hard times - know that. Be joyful in hope, patient in affliction, and faithful in prayer. Prayer works. I had a praying mother, and yes, she saw me through my time of drug abuse. She never stopped praying. She never stops helping, and she never stops believing.

The Almighty is strategic in all his ways. Even in opposition, God is creating opportunity. There may be times when things seem to be going in the wrong direction and need to increase, but you see a decrease. Stay hopeful. God does not always take us in the way we planned; it may be uncomfortable, and sometimes you may have to come off the mountain. You may even take a detour in the valley only to elevate yourself to something greater. Remember God's ways and thoughts are not like ours. His plans are good and not evil. Always know that we are required to keep hoping in our Savior no matter what we may face. He will save us spiritually and naturally.

Keep trusting Him and believe that as it says in Philippians 1:6, *being confident of this, that he who began a good work in you will carry it on to completion until the day of Christ Jesus.*

That trying part of my life caused me to go into the jails and minister to others, be an encourager to those I have come in contact with and speak to many different men and women. I'm a minister of the gospel and also a certified Peer Recovery Coach, an opportunity that gives me great joy - teaching and helping to inspire others through the process of addiction.

I encourage you to use what you've been through and know that this journey is not only about you but it is about helping others along their journey as well. In the words of Reverend Jesse Jackson, "Keep hope alive."

NICOLE DIXSON-MAYS

Nicole Dixson-Mays is the innovator, motivator, and mentor for women. She is passionate about offering HOPE to the people of God through the Word. That infectious smile blesses everyone that encounters her. Her voice soothes when she ministers in song and worship. She is a wife and has a beautiful twenty-five-year-old daughter. She is a certified nurse aide and Peer Recovery Coach.

Hope is favorable and confident expectation; it's an expectant attitude that something good is going to happen and things will work out, no matter what situation we're facing.- **Joyce Meyer**

WRITING HOPE & IMAGINING TOMORROW

Honestly, I am still blown away by how I'm a three-time award-winning writer and producer. I am the first guest editor of my college's alumni magazine. I am an author who wrote my first book at the age of six. I work for one of the most well-known literary organizations in the country, and I have moved hundreds of writers into action and audiences to tears for over fifteen years.

But there was a time when I underestimated the power of storytelling. Case in point...

Early February 2020, my partner-in-rhyme and I performed at a festival with our show, *HERstory of HIStory*. When I pulled up at the suburban school, I noticed three things: (1) the size of the campus was like nothing I had ever seen before; there were several well-maintained buildings, large parking lots, and an extended winding entrance; (2) the student body population was fairly diverse; and (3) even within that diversity, the number of Black students was still a handful.

During the last show, I felt a kinship with one of the Black students who decided to sit in the front row. I wanted to let her know that I saw her, so I locked eyes with this young woman, and we engaged in an unspoken communion.

After the show, she waited for everybody else to leave, and I stood there patiently as she scanned the room. When the last student left, I noticed her bottom lip begin to quiver. Her eyes also rolled in the back of her head like she was trying to stop a rushing train. One word fell from her mouth, the first tear dropped, and I knew what was coming my way.

For this young sophomore, I was the first Black educator she had ever seen and the first time she saw someone up on the stage telling her story. She saw her reflection for the first time.

At that moment, this student released every cruel joke her peers let fall from their mouths, every hesitation she had when someone asked to touch her hair, every piece of false information she read in her textbooks. Our connection took me back to when I was the "only" in my predominantly white college classroom and the weight I carried for four years. I was lucky enough to have someone reassure me of my experiences; however, I was her first salvation.

Has there ever been a time when you were an "only" in a space? I want you to remember the feeling and think about the weight you carried with you being so isolated. I want you to recall when you finally saw your reflection in a movie, story, on stage, or in a play. I want you to be in *that* moment. What did that sigh of relief feel like in your body when you realized you were not alone?

At that moment, this young lady was able to see herself for the first time, and we were able to talk about all the things that come with being in this skin. My storytelling opened up a door and liberated her from the isolation.

My words were what she had been trying to articulate for years. She now had a container for her experiences, and my truth gave her hope.

So, I have a question for you, when was the last time you gave someone hope through your story? Have you had the opportunity to share where you've come from, and you ignored it? Has there ever been a time when you said, "I am not a writer, "or "I don't have enough time," or "I can't write like Toni Morrison or Te-Nehisi Coates"?

If you've ever held onto this thought for more than a second, then, let's be real, you are the one getting in your way. Hmm. Your trepidation is holding you back from the hope your story can provide.

Well, you might say, "But Heather, I wasn't born with the creative gene."

Here is where you let go of your preconceived notions of what it means to be creative and create your definition.

For me, creativity is the ability to fly above traditional ideas and create new ones. Creativity is the opportunity to grow something new with your fingerprint. Creativity is the space between what we see and what we *hope* for, dream about, and imagine for the world. What's your definition?

I am sure there has been a time when you imagined a new scenario or hoped for something better. So - Create. Imagine. Hope. Spread your wings and dive into a story.

Need examples?

How about 50 years ago, when Marie Van Brittan Brown didn't feel safe in her home, in Queens, when her husband was gone. So they decided to drill peepholes into their front door and inserted a camera so she could monitor the outside. This system was later patented and sold and transformed into what we now know as the security system.

Thirty years ago, we didn't have smartphones. Fifty years ago, we didn't have the internet. One hundred and twenty years ago, anyone who was a Black woman couldn't vote. Someone had to imagine something better, something new. These stories belong to other people, but they can inspire us to tell our own.

My question to you then is, what will you imagine? How will you ignite your creativity so you can instill hope and inspire others?

My way is through storytelling, and as storytellers, we can translate existing ideas into new sources of inspiration for others. I believe we have a duty to share our stories with the world. What's your story?

Fun fact: I fondly refer to my community as HummingByrds - a combination being the actual birds and the healing properties of humming. Hummingbirds are natural pollinators. They feed and transport seeds to other flowers, constantly creating something new and naturally becoming part of the process. Hummingbirds are messengers.

My question to you is, what is your message? What do you want to share? Who are you sending it to? How are you providing hope for the next person who is going to read about your story?

The humming part of "HummingByrds" refers to the intentional vibrational pattern you send out into the world that has a rippling effect. We can use humming as a form of healing. Through humming, we learn to use our voice as a tool of empowerment.

What if you realize you could be in charge of your healing journey. Hmm. Let's practice the power of humming.

Right now, close your eyes, and I want you to inhale and count to three, and when you exhale, you will do so with a great hum. You want to send that hum to a specific part of your body that needs it the most. When you hum, I want you to IMAGINE chipping away at something you were dealing with in your life that needs to be dismantled or recalibrated. Send the hum there with intention. Now, take a deep breath, inhale, and hum.

Hmmm.

Now that you have realigned yourself let's take a look at a few steps to help you master creativity and ignite your inner creativity with your story.

First, accept your place in the world as a HummingByrd, a messenger of hope, joy, and possibility to heal others through your vibrational pattern. You have a message inside of you. Recognize it, draft it, and share it. You have a boulder in your belly, and it's begging you to leap so your wings will appear. Trust it.

Second, nurture yourself and set up your space so your mind is ready to work. Hummingbirds are energy workers, which means they need to constantly refuel themselves with nectar to continue to move through the world. You, my dear future writer, have the opportunity to be an energy worker through writing and storytelling, and you need the right inspiration to get work out into the world. As yourself, how can you be a healthier messenger?

- o Open up your throat chakras by eating blueberries or dragon fruit. You can also add eucalyptus, spearmint, peppermint, or cypress to your oil diffuser.
- o Practice the humming exercise we did earlier at least five times a day.
- o Repeat to yourself, "I have a story to tell" ten times a day in the mirror every morning.

Third, START WRITING TODAY. NO EXCUSES. Carve out time, preferably in the morning, and write at least twenty minutes every day. Writing in the morning will help release any thoughts bogging you down, so you have a clearer mind. If you can take the time at night, you can reflect on your day.

Finally, make a list of at least ten small things that nurture you or provide you with your inspiration and commit to completing this list over a month.

You have the tools to leap into creative action. Nothing is holding you back from birthing your extraordinary story. Remember, you are a writer, and you are creative. You have a book inside of you, and you've put that book off for long enough. It's time to set aside your fears. Scan the QR Code to receive your free resource today to help your brainstorm further on how you can unlock your creative blocks.

HummingByrds take flight, and you, future writer, are a  HummingByrd. I am here to tell you; you are not alone. I see you. I invite you to uncover all the stories buried in your bones. Let's find a way to realign your creative path so *YOU* can be in joy, ignite creativity, spread your wings, and fly.

Besides being an award-winning writer and producer, Heather, aka 'Byrd,' has over 15 years of experience as a creative catalyst. She uses her experiences to help invisible voices be heard. She is an entrepreneur, speaker, and educator for one of the largest literary nonprofits in the country. She is the author of *Mahogany, A Letter to Black*, available on Amazon.

You can reach her at https://www.byrdsworld.com/contact

CARLA MARIA ALLEN

Carla Maria Allen fulfilled her dream and graduated from Wayne State University with a bachelor's degree in Education. She worked five years in the classroom teaching children and three years in Administration as the Title One Facilitator. Carla holds a master's degree in Special Education with the concentration area of Learning Disabilities.

God had impressed upon her spirit from when she was a little girl to implement a Christian School. With God's help and the numerous prophetic words to confirm this, she has placed in motion the beginning stages to see this school implemented and opening soon. She intends to help educate children to love God and have a solid educational background to help them live according to 3 John 1:2, which states, "I wish above all things that you may prosper and be in health, even as your souls prosper."

Carla resides in Michigan with the joy of her life, husband, Pastor Gilbert L. Allen. They have two adult children and two grandchildren.

 Evangelist Carla Allen and her upcoming book will be available in 2022..

For more info on her ministry:
https://www.greaterlifeapostolic.net/co-pastor-carla-allen.html

BRIGITTE BROWN JACKSON

Brigitte Jackson, Ed. S is an Evangelist and minister of the gospel for Kingdom Influence Global Ministries. As the Editor in Chief for Ubuntu Press, Brigitte published this anthology of stories to provide others with the similar hope she was given in some of the darkest moments of her life by influential female mentors.

An accomplished leadership strategist and motivational speaker, Brigitte founded Exponential EduVentures, a professional development firm that serves individual clients and organizations. Leading multi-million-dollar organizations since 2005, Brigitte has personally managed hundreds of people. As a consultant, she has trained various groups on leadership, self-esteem, resilience, group dynamics, teamwork, accountability, and communication skills for the past two decades. Brigitte is a certified Extreme Execution Coach, Innermetrix DISC consultant. She is married to Willie Don Jackson, III. They have 8 children and 11 grandchildren and currently reside in Michigan.

Brigitte is the host of the podcast, Powerful, available on Apple podcasts, Amazon Music, iHeart Radio, and all major podcast platforms. You can also listen at https://brigittebrownjackson.com/podcast.

She can be followed on LinkedIn at Brigitte Brown Jackson and Facebook and Instagram @BrigitteTransforms

Learn more about Brigitte at www.brigittebrownjackson.com

GET YOUR FREE EBOOK

https://brigittebrownjackson.com/free-pdf

GET YOUR FULL-SERVICE PUBLISHING NEEDS

WWW.UBUNTUPRESS.COM

WHEN YOU PURCHASE

POWERFUL: GROW IN YOU & UNLOCK YOUR PURPOSE

YOU RECEIVE A GIFT VALUED AT $397.00

REGULAR $99

TEXT THE WORD 'BOOK' TO (810) 321-5365

FIND OUT HOW TO GET INTRODUCTORY PRICE

PARABLE OF THE TALENTS

MATTHEW 25:14-27

14 "Again, it will be like a man going on a journey, who called his servants and entrusted his wealth to them. 15 To one he gave five bags of gold, to another two bags, and to another one bag,[a] each according to his ability. Then he went on his journey. 16 The man who had received five bags of gold went at once and put his money to work and gained five bags more. 17 So also, the one with two bags of gold gained two more. 18 But the man who had received one bag went off, dug a hole in the ground and hid his master's money. 21 "His master replied, 'Well done, good and faithful servant! You have been faithful with a few things; I will put you in charge of many things. Come and share your master's happiness!' 22 "The man with two bags of gold also came. 'Master,' he said, 'you entrusted me with two bags of gold; see, I have gained two more.' 23 "His master replied, 'Well done, good and faithful servant! You have been faithful with a few things; I will put you in charge of many things. Come and share your master's happiness!' 24 "Then the man who had received one bag of gold came. 'Master,' he said, 'I knew that you are a hard man, harvesting where you have not sown and gathering where you have not scattered seed. 25 So I was afraid and went out and hid your gold in the ground. See, here is what belongs to you.' 26 "His master replied, 'You wicked, lazy servant! So you knew that I harvest where I have not sown and gather where I have not scattered seed? 27 Well then, you should have put my money on deposit with the bankers, so that when I returned, I would have received it back with interest.

> *When I stand before God at the end of my life, I would hope that I would not have a single bit of talent left, and could say, 'I used everything you gave me'.*
> Erma Bombeck

Made in the USA
Coppell, TX
27 September 2021